D0466006

HE'S GONE...
YOU'RE BACK

The Right Way to Get Over Mr. Wrong

KERIKA FIELDS

Afterword by Janeula M. Burt, PhD

SOULS OF MY SISTERS BOOKS

Kensington Publishing Corp.

http://www.kensingtonbooks.com

SOULS OF MY SISTERS books are published by

Kensington Publishing Corp. and Souls of My Sisters, Inc.
850 Third Avenue
New York, NY 10022

All Kensington titles, imprints and distributed lines are available at special quantity discounts for bulk purchases for sales promotion, premiums, fund-raising, educational or institutional use.

Special book excerpts or customized printings can also be created to fit specific needs. For details, write or phone the office of the Kensington Special Sales Manager: Attn. Special Sales Department, Kensington Publishing Corp., 850 Third Avenue, New York, NY 10022. Phone: 1-800-221-2647.

ISBN-13: 978-0-7582-2958-8
ISBN-10: 0-7582-2958-5

First Trade Paperback Printing: January 2009
10 9 8 7 6 5 4 3 2 1

Printed in the United States of America

This book is dedicated to the memories of my cousins Ayofemi Richards, Robert Conner, and Cole Blaze. You are gone but not forgotten. Your beauty, kindness, and strength are always with me. So glad to have known you. So glad you were ours, mine, for a time.

Acknowledgments

This book has been a long time coming and is a result of my many experiences, life lessons, and personal and professional trials and triumphs. It wasn't easy, but I made it through the darkness to the other side where there is light. I will never look back.

Thank you, God, for always being there and for never leaving me even when I was ready to cut out on myself. I am a witness to your power and glory. Please continue to bless me with your grace.

I am also thankful to all the men I've loved before, for teaching me about myself, showing me my strengths and weaknesses, and forcing me to grow. I am especially thankful to You (and you know who you are) for loving me enough to let me go. I guess it was for the best after all.

But this book is not for you. This book is for my sisters Keina, Kidada, Adenike, Nairobi, Vici, Angela, Corliss, Damia, Helen, Jackie, Jewel, Jodi, Joyce, Lydia, Mekita, Nicole, Odette, Sheila, Tamika, Terrell, Hattie (both of you), and all of those who have laughed with me, cried with me, prayed with me, and grown with me. Come fly with me!

I would also like to thank my Sacred Sisters from the winter class of 2003. We are the ones who made it through the storm! I will never forget the experience and am forever grateful to Queen Afua for teaching me the truth and for showing me my seat (the challenge now is to stay on it, but at least I know it's there).

Special shout-out to my She Shootin' Sisters—Ava, Delphine, Laylah, and Nsenga—for keeping me focused and inspiring me to keep taking pictures, to continue to capture life's fleeting moments, beautiful faces, and unique places.

I want to thank the women who had a hand in bringing this book forth: Gwendolyn Quinn of Mighty Quinn Management (you push my buttons, but you also keep me on my toes. I hate to admit it, but I need you); Candace Sandy and Dawn Marie Daniels of Souls of My Sisters (so glad you were clear enough to know a good thing when you saw it! I'm talking about me and my book! Thank you for being believers); Kensington Publishing Corp.: Walter and Steven Zacharius, Laurie Parkin, Rakia Clark, and Kristine Noble. Thank you, Dr. Janeula Burt, for writing the afterword. Last but not least, Marie Brown, who saw my potential in the very beginning. Thank you for all of your advice and encouragement over the years.

Special thanks and blessings go to my daughter, the one and only Skye West, for tolerating my moods, making my teas, and giving me good hugs when I need them the most. You are growing beautifully, and I am so proud of the girl you are and the woman you are becoming. I pray that all your dreams come true and that you always love yourself first and foremost. I know that you will fall in love and experience heartache (it's an inevitable part of life, baby), but I also know that you will surely survive thanks to your strength, courage, wisdom, and the words in this book. Use this tool whenever you get lost. You are my true target audience.

My Mama Natelege—I hope you know that I would not be as creative and conscious if you were not my mother. I am so grateful for you and your influence on me. I hope I make you proud.

My Marilyn—God knew I needed more than one mother, so he gave me two—the other is you!

Aunt Addie, Aunt Bibi, Aunt Fannie, Aunt Amaka, and Aunt Aisha: You know I love you. You know I need you. Always have. Always will.

Grandma Marie, you never cease to amaze me. I will make every effort to be as strong, stylish, sassy, resilient, generous, and wise as you have been all of your life. You are our family jewel; you give us value and make all that we have been through together—the good and the bad, the births and the deaths—strengthening.

My brothers Akiyomi and Rajani for being shining examples that strong, smart, spiritual Black men do exist. Stay strong. We need you.

And in the end, as always, is my dear old dad, Rogers, who is there for me no matter what. I do appreciate you, even if I don't always show it. I hope you know this is only the beginning.

Contents

Introduction

THE ONE

My mother always told my three sisters and me, "Girls, I'll give you one!" She was firm. She was straightforward. She was serious. "Everybody gets their heart broken in life," she assured us, "but after that first big one, you learn. After that, you know what you're getting yourself into when you fall in love. You know the chances you take for the love you make." She assured us she'd always be there for us no matter what and no matter how many times we had our hearts broken. But she admitted she'd only really sympathize with and support one: one disappointment, one devastation, one broken heart.

Well, for me there has been more than one heartbreak, bad boyfriend, painfully disappointing love relationship. But yes, just like my mother predicted, there was that one. The one who taught me the pleasure of love and the pain of loss. The one who grew me up and erased the childish fantasy that learning to love another and accepting the love of another is ever easy.

He had light brown eyes, hazel some would say, and a loud, booming, infectious laugh. He was five feet eleven inches tall, with a clear, almond-colored complexion.

I can't remember the first time I ever saw him or the first time we really met because technically he's my godbrother (seriously!!). His mother and my mother worked at a shoe store together when they were both young and married and pregnant, and became fast friends. So as kids we went to each other's baptisms and birthday parties and all that jazz. We even ended up going to the same high school, but he was a year ahead of me since he was skipped and hung out with a totally different crowd. So I rarely saw him, and when I did, he was running raucously through the hallways. I wasn't paying any attention to him anyway; I was a funny and popular girl with my own so-called social life. We would nod to one another and pass on the occasional mother-to-mother message, but for the most part he was insignificant and invisible. That is, until I saw him. I mean, really saw him.

It was a few years after high school, and I decided to drop in on my mother. I probably needed money or something, and I expected she'd be home, ready to lecture me about being more financially responsible. I didn't expect he'd be standing there, in her kitchen, in an apron, his usually askew dreadlocks pulled neatly in a bunch, revealing his smooth, sweet complexion; pink, full lips; and those pretty brown eyes. It was all over for me right then and there. It was love at first sight. I was literally blinded by his beauty, because all I could see was fine and pretty, not unstable and a little crazy.

We started hanging out on and off. We'd go to 125th Street in Harlem in its heyday and buy books, jewelry, and incense. We'd go to lectures at the Schomburg and student art exhibits at CUNY. I was in a trance, lost in his eyes and caught up on his every word. He was intelligent and inspiring and unlike any guy I'd ever been around. After all, he was from the 'hood—the Queensbridge housing projects—and I was a Brooklyn Brownstone Bohemian. We existed in our own little blissful bubble. It was beautiful. But then it got ugly. "What's wrong with you, you fat bitch?!" he yelled at me six weeks after I gave birth to our beautiful daughter. I was in shock, but I really shouldn't have been.

Just years previously, when we went to visit his mother in her small but well-decorated apartment, he revealed a side of himself that I should have taken seriously. I sat and talked to his mom while he ran to the store to pick up some things for her from a list she'd made. It was a regular ritual for the two of them, as he would go visit her to run her errands as much as he could due to the fact that she was handicapped. She'd lost part of her leg when she fell in the subway tracks on her way to the doctor while pregnant with him, had part of her leg run over, and had lived to tell the tale.

That day I asked her if there was anything she needed me to do; I couldn't possibly, under the circumstances, expect her to cater to me or accept her offer to fix me tea or whatever. She asked me to press her hair, and I obliged; growing up with three sisters, you learn your way around a straightening comb. As I stood over her, pressing her hair while we chitchatted, he came through the door and had a fit. He started yelling at the top of his lungs at the both of us, first asking me what the fu— I thought I was doing. When I told him his mother had asked me to press her hair, he turned his wrath on her, telling her that she was brainwashed by white society and watched too much television, that she needed to leave her hair alone. He insulted her, saying, "You're never going to look like those women on television, no matter what you do!" I tried to remind him that his mother was grown and if she chose to press her hair that was her business. He told me to shut up and went on insulting his mother in the most incredible ways. She was a hypocrite. She was a fool. Then he hit below the belt, telling her that he understood now why his father left, why he never wanted to be around her or, consequently, him.

I should have known right there and then that he had some unresolved, deep-seeded issues with his mother, his situation, and himself. But I was young and evidently dumb. Besides, we had been together for a few years, and I'd never seen that side of him. I chalked it up to a bad mood and moved on—and in with him a few months later!—only to be, of course, cursed out for dear life my damn self. But what did I really expect? If he could curse out his crippled mother, what made me think he would spare me? I guess I wasn't paying attention when Maya Angelou so famously said, "When someone shows you who they are, believe them."

I couldn't believe it, though. As I was standing in our living room after just breastfeeding the baby, in he walks with those words. I admit I was heavy, but I had just given birth. Besides, everybody knows one thing you don't call a Black woman, under any circumstance, is fat. Big-boned. Thick. But fat?! Oh hells no!!

I remember a girlfriend of mine telling me a story about how her mother felt about the word. Growing up in the South, she and her brothers would walk barefoot to school while the white kids rode the bus and taunted them, calling them pickaninnies, jigaboos, and of course the inevitable N-word. The little girl would just ignore the insults as she trudged her way through the bushes. But one day one of them said something she could not and would not ignore. "Hey there, little fat n—r!" one of them called out to her. "Who you calling fat?!!" she demanded before pelting the bus with a handful of rocks. You see, because all that other stuff was expected. But fat? Them was fighting words!!

But seriously, his was a hurtful form of verbal abuse that only got worse until one day I decided I couldn't take it any-more. My daughter was eighteen months, walking and just beginning to talk. It was clear he was not going to edit, cor-rect, or clean up his speech. It was clear I couldn't live that way, with someone going off on me at any given moment. I mean, I'm strong, but I'm a sensitive thing, and one thing I couldn't take was getting cursed out in the daytime and mo-lested at night (which is basically what it is when you are not feeling someone but oblige just to get it over and done with so you can get some sleep before the baby wakes up). Plus, I grew up in a household where my father yelled—a lot. My nerves were already bad. I felt like I was about to lose my mind, and the one thing I cherish above all else—above my beauty, above my creativity—is my sanity.

So I told him he had to move out. We had already broken up and gotten back together a few times, and I was tired. Tired of him. Tired of us. I tried to stick it out, though, because of the baby. But I always knew deep down that we would not end up together in the long run. I mean, when I told him I was pregnant, he said, "Well, I guess that means you wanna get married, huh, 'Rika?" I sucked my teeth and said, "No, that does not mean I want to get married," simply because I knew that was not what my marriage proposal was supposed to sound like, and if he knew me, he would have known at least that.

There were other telltale signs our union was not to be. When I was pregnant, I would ask him to smoke outside. Instead, he would go into the other room and leave the door open as I lay alone in the bed. I would rub my stomach and say to my baby, "It's me and you, kid. It's me and you." Still, I stuck it out. I wanted my daughter to know her father. Despite his issues, he is an extremely unique and intelligent man, whom she deserved to have in her life. But once I really realized that it was no longer working for me, that there was no way I was going to raise my daughter in a verbally abusive relationship, all the shit hit the fan. For real. He told me he would leave when he was good and ready. I demanded to know when that would be, and he told me when he friggin' felt like it! Frustrated, I pushed him with both hands on his shoulders, and he fell into the closet. I must admit it was kinda funny. I thought I'd stifled my giggle, but he must have seen it because he was infuriated. He lifted his hand up to hit me and stopped it midair. He had to know that if he hit me, that would surely be the end. With all of our disagreements and fights during our seven-year relationship, he had never hit me, never put his hands on me. And it was a good thing, too, because I'd told him that was the one thing I would not and could not deal with—especially after growing up in a house where I would hear my parents argue at night only to wake up in the morning and watch my mother putting on big seventies shades to hide her big black eye.

Our entire relationship flashed before my eyes in the five seconds that his hand was in the air. The way we used to be. How much fun we had together. How he took care of me while I was pregnant and was there every step of the way in the delivery room. How he looked when he first held our daughter. How he cried when his sister died. For those five seconds, there was hope. There was a chance we might have been able to work things out if he went to anger management. There was a possibility that we could have raised our daughter together. Alas, it was not to be, because seconds after he stopped himself, he let it all go—our love, our family, our future. "Pow!!" was all I heard as his big man hand—the hand that had held mine in many a movie, the hand that had rubbed oil on my belly when I was pregnant, the hand that I had kissed when we made love—came crashing down on the entire left side of my pretty little face. After that, there was nothing. Everything was silent. Our relationship was officially over. That simple slap was *my* Point of No Return (see Chapter 1).

Even though I was miserable when he was there, I was numb when he was gone. What the hell was I supposed to do, alone, with a baby? How was I going to survive or even thrive out in the cold, cruel world? Would anyone else ever love me again? Would I ever love anyone again? Yeah, a lot of questions go through your head when you're alone in an apartment with a crying baby.

Thankfully, though, the answers started to come. My numbness began to thaw. I decided that I would embrace his absence—I really did want him out, after all—and use it to make me better. I had been taking care of him, a baby, and a household. So I started taking care of me. And it felt good, right, and long overdue. Because truth be told—I *was* a fat bitch!! I had only lost fifteen of the sixty pounds I had gained during my pregnancy. I wasn't doing the things I loved—wasn't writing, wasn't taking pictures (except of the baby), wasn't enjoying the New York art scene—so I was cranky, agitated, and mad. But once I was alone, I realized who I was mad at: I was mad at me for letting myself go, for deferring my dreams, for loving a man more than I loved myself! I mean, when had it become more important to make him a full-course meal than to take my behind to the gym, or for a walk, or to a dance class, or out dancing with friends? I was flabbergasted but strangely freed because I had learned many valuable lessons that changed me for life. The beautiful thing is that it changed me for the better. It made me stronger. Smarter. And gave me my Skye (that's our daughter), and for that, no matter what we went through or how much I was hurt, I will be forever grateful for the experience.

I was forced to pull it together, suck it up, and get on with my life. I had to find out who I really was and what really made me happy. I had to stand on my own two feet, face my faults, and find my strengths. I had to Avoid the Abyss (see Chapter 3) by taking care of myself the best way I possibly could. And I learned that I didn't need a lot of money or fancy doctors or an expensive spa trip (although it would have been nice!) to cleanse myself, pamper myself, heal myself. I created and embraced my own Recipes for Recovery (see Chapter 6) and discovered that a little lemon water, a big cup of tea, continual prayer, and a whole bunch of fresh fruit and green vegetables can go a long way, baby!

Everything I learned, I'm sharing here with you, my broken-hearted, disillusioned, depressed, debilitated sister friends. I want you to get over it and get on with your life. I want you to be healthy, happy, and fly. Now when I say fly, I don't mean it only in the way we are accustomed to—referring to each other as fly if we look good, have our hair tight, have the latest shoes and the most expensive bag. That's all fine and good. But know that when I say I want you and me—us—to be fly, what I mean is this: a fly woman is flying. Her spirit soars. She has laid her burdens down and has risen above all of her adversities. She has earned her wings. It's a major accomplishment for any woman—especially one who has survived a broken heart. We throw the word around a lot, but I want to give it a whole new meaning. I want to re-assess and reinvent what it really means to be fly. Being fly is not only about looking good—but you know how we do it, ladies! Being fly is about having yourself and your life together on every level. Your mind is right. Your health is on point. Your money situation is straight. Your spiritual life is strong. To me, that's what I call fly. So, the next time you call someone fly or consider yourself fly, make sure you take into account all the elements of being fly. You know why? Because he's gone, you're back!!!

Chapter 1

THE POINT OF NO RETURN

"I am not afraid of storms, for I am learning how to sail my ship." Louisa May Alcott

You know it immediately when you get there—to that point in your relationship where there is no turning back, when you finally see your relationship for what it was, not what you wanted it to be, when you are forced to face the fact that the relationship is not working and you have to move on. Alone. It's a very painful place, this point of no return. The pain is so numbing, startling, and piercing that you cannot ignore it. Because up until this point you figured that you could make the relationship work, had convinced yourself that he (or you) would change, that things would miraculously be different, that he was The One, this was it, the love of your life, and love conquers all, even lies, neglect, abuse, abandonment, fear of commitment, substance abuse, infidelity, indifference, and unaccountability.

When that moment comes, you know it immediately, regardless of what happened to bring you there. It is a moment of immeasurable clarity, because it contrasts with the continual noise in your mind, the questions, doubts, hopes, and fears. It just is. The Truth. It is over. And there is no turning back.

It may have been a long time coming, and even though you knew that eventually it would have to end, that you would have to walk away, you didn't let yourself think about when exactly the end would come. You said things to yourself like *this can't be happening; I can make it work*, etc. But when you reach the point of no return, your self-talk changes effortlessly, through no attempt of your own. You just stop and hear this: "I cannot do this anymore." Period. There are no excuses, no explanations. Just fact. "I need to leave this man alone," your inner voice says. And you are calm. "I cannot survive if I stay in this place with this person." And you take a deep, cleansing breath. "He is not the one for me." And you see, finally, that it is so true. Then there's that so sad yet simple statement: "I'm done." And you are.

And it didn't even really hurt, yet, because at that point, in that moment, you were anesthetized by the truth. The tears that did eventually, inevitably fall were not fast, erratic tears. No, this time they were hot, heavy, and slow. You felt each individual crystal teardrop as it formed in your heart, moved past your chest, then traveled up inside the back of your throat until it reached the inside corner of your eye, where it teetered, only for a moment, before it fell, full and hot, almost burning your delicate face as it rolled down the side of your nose, slowly taking its time to reach the rim of your top lip, where it sat still once more, pausing before its trip to its final destination, that place called your tongue, where you discovered that its saltiness was somewhat bittersweet. Yes, because, you see, these were not the tears of a woman in the wrong relationship; these were the tears of a liberated woman, a woman who is no longer in denial or in limbo, a woman who has let go because she has had a moment of clarity about her situation, an epiphany of sorts, and she can see that no amount of crying, begging, talking, drinking, sexing, lying, or praying will make it work.

Now, instead of working on your relationship, you will be working on yourself. Instead of nurturing him, you prepare to nurture you. Instead of wracking your brain trying to figure out what will make him happy, you figure out what makes you happy. What do *you* want to do with the rest of *your* life? What kind of lifestyle do *you* want to live? These are important questions, especially because we tend to make many sacrifices and compromises in relationships. And for the most part that is expected and commended. Love is a two-way street—give-and-take is mandatory in any relationship. Unfortunately, since women are by nature more nurturing than men, we tend to give more than we get, and we don't even notice it until the relationship is over, until we've reached the point of no return.

Believe it or not, the point of no return is a really beautiful place to be. You've made it through the turbulent times of struggle, the doubt, the questions, the suspicions, and the insecurities. Now you are on solid ground. Your feet are planted firmly in a hard but necessary place called reality.

The point of no return is a very personal place. Regardless of what has happened in the relationship in the past, or what wrongs you feel have been done to you, regardless of disappointment and distrust, or having your heart broken over and over and over again by the same person, there will come a point when you will say enough is enough. No matter how many times you tell yourself that you have to, that you must move on, no matter how many ways your mother, your sister, or your best friend says you should leave the relationship, tells you he's no good, he doesn't love you, you deserve better, etc., etc., etc., it is you and only you who can, and will, decide when the relationship is truly over. And no matter how many times you've forgiven him, taken him back, suppressed your true feelings for the sake of saving the relationship, the time will come when you will KNOW that it is over. And you WILL move on. But when you do, it will be your decision. NO ONE, nothing, can tell you any different until you reach that point, that powerful, pivotal point that only you will experience, that only you can define.

The point of no return is always a different place for different people. He may come home late one too many times, and ignore, hit, or insult you for the last time. It really depends on how much you, and only you, can take or are willing to tolerate. Some women put up with verbal abuse for years only to leave—and rightfully so!—once the abuse turns physical. Some women cannot tolerate verbal abuse at all, on any level, at any time, from any man. Some women choose to look the other way if they know their man is cheating; others do not. So yeah, it's personal. It basically depends on your individual level of tolerance. What bothers you, disturbs you, or sets you off may do nothing for the next woman. What gets you to that place where you can't go back? Sometimes all it takes is the wrong glance, the indifferent attitude, or something as simple as the wrong word. A hurtful word or a slap out of nowhere or an inexplicable insult is easy to recognize and they are understandable triggers of a relationship's demise. They are jolting incidents that shock you, then help you see.

I had a friend whose live-in boyfriend was the sweetest man she'd ever met—in the beginning. Then, after they'd moved in together, she realized his casual drinking wasn't that casual and his occasional drug use was happening more than occasionally. She even discovered he had nightmares that she had to carefully coax him out of. But she loved him. So she kept him. Everybody told her she was crazy if she couldn't see he was crazy and encouraged her to end the relationship. But she didn't. She was convinced he made her happy and was willing to tolerate his many issues, until she called me crying one day, saying that she'd told him to move out. She couldn't take it anymore. She had reached her point of no return. Of course I was extremely curious about what he could have done, after all he'd already done, to make her get to that point, to make her make him leave. Did he hit her? Sleep with her coworker? Steal money? No. It was something much more simple, but to her, much more hurtful: he called her a cunt. That one, ill-chosen word blew her mind and blew the relationship wide apart. To this day, she cannot remember what the discussion was about nor the argument that resulted from the discussion. All she can remember is that word—cunt. They had been going back and forth in an effort to resolve their many issues and many things were said. But that word stopped her cold in her tracks. She was immobilized by its implications. She had been called many things in her day, but never that. And to be called that by a man whom she loved dearly, whom she opened her heart, home, and legs to (let's keep it real, ladies), was all the more devastating. The moment he said that word to her face, she realized how he really saw her, how he really felt. She couldn't excuse it away. With one ugly word, this Queen of Denial relinquished her crown to the reality of the man she was living with.

For the record, this friend wasn't the only Queen of Denial I knew. In fact, I've known many and have been a Queen of Denial myself at one point or another—walking around with my head held high, refusing to look down and around at what was really going on in my relationship. It's what a Queen of Denial does best—denies anything is wrong, denies the relationship is suffering or, as in my case, denies it is doomed from the start.

A few years ago I met a guy who was sweet and sincere and soulful. He was also ten years younger than I was, recently divorced, working odd jobs, and living in a room. He was in a transitional phase of his life, starting over, figuring things out. I was a grown woman working on my already established career and raising a child. Still, I believed him when he said that he was ready for a serious relationship, that he knew what he wanted, that what he wanted was me, us. So for six months I pretended it was really going to work—despite the fact that he was young, confused, and broke. I acted like all I needed was love, that it didn't matter if he didn't have any money and could do absolutely nothing for me. I pretended that I didn't know that someone who was recently divorced was in no real condition to jump into another relationship. I convinced myself that the age difference didn't matter and wasn't an issue when, for me, at that time, it was. I even got mad at my best friend for bringing these issues up to me and got even madder when, at a party, she went up to him and basically told him not to play with my heart, to make sure he knew what he was doing because she didn't want to see her friend hurt (again).

In the end, she was right, and my boyfriend and I both ended up hurt. He wasn't ready for me, wasn't anywhere on my level, and definitely didn't know what he wanted out of life. It ended up being a painful experience that I could have avoided if only I wasn't a Queen of Denial, if only I hadn't lied to myself about what I wanted out of a relationship and where he was in his life. I did learn a lot about myself from the relationship and have forgiven myself for denying myself the truth of what I wanted, needed, and deserved from an intimate relationship. Plus, I know I'm not the only one. I know there are way too many Queens of Denial out there, so beware. Sometimes they are not so easy to see. But because I've been one, I find Queens of Denial simple to spot:

✦ A Queen of Denial will get angry if you approach her about obvious problems in her relationship.

✦ A Queen of Denial rarely discusses details of her relationship with anyone, even her closest friends.

✦ If she has, in some rare moment of weakness or clarity, mentioned trouble in the relationship and you ask how it's going, a Queen of Denial will lie to you—and herself—saying everything is fine.

✦ A Queen of Denial doesn't look you in the eye when she tells you how happy she is.

✦ A Queen of Denial makes excuses for her man's whereabouts, bad behavior, or disrespect.

✦ A Queen of Denial goes out of her way to make the relationship appear to be something other than it is.

✦ A Queen of Denial thinks her outward appearance is more important than her inner state of being.

✦ A Queen of Denial does most of the work required to keep the relationship together.

✦ A Queen of Denial is deathly afraid to face the truth about her relationship, because if she does, then she will have to relinquish her crown, and she will no longer be allowed to live in fantasy land; she will be forced to live out her days with the rest of us, in a place called reality.

As you look at this list, I know you may know a few Queens of Denial in your world. Like the friend who's always acting like her relationship is all of that when everyone—including her—knows her man is a chronic cheater. Or the coworker who has been engaged for years, loves to show off her engagement ring, but still can't tell you exactly when the wedding will be. It's sad, because Queens of Denial suffer for their obliviousness. Take, for example, our girl Jennifer Hudson's character in the movie *Dreamgirls*, Effie White. Now there was a Queen of Denial who suffered. Curtis Taylor was a hustler and player, but she didn't mind. She could handle it. She basically threw herself at him, claimed him as her man (he never claimed her), turned a blind eye to the fact that he was clearly infatuated with Deena, convinced herself that he was instead in love with her, then was surprised and hurt when he unsympathetically ended their business and personal relationship in one move. After all of that, she still wasn't having it, and she told him, told him, that he was going to love her indeed. Wow. Now I'm not being unsympathetic. I loved the movie and was in awe of Ms. Hudson's performance, even though it could never compare to that of Jennifer Holiday in the Broadway play, which I was fortunate enough to see live as a child. It's just that Effie White was the ultimate Queen of Denial. But she was just a character in a movie. There are, unfortunately, Queens of Denial everywhere, walking around every day, pretending that everything is all right.

It's sometimes easy to see Queen of Denial traits in others, but can you see these traits in yourself? If you are honest with yourself, I think you'd agree that you have also been a Queen of Denial at one point or another. Have you ever lied to yourself about the state of a relationship? Have you ever lied to family and friends about a relationship issue? Have you ever convinced yourself that you were willing and able to deal with a situation in a relationship when in fact you were not? If so, you have been a Queen of Denial. But it's okay. Women often turn into Queens of Denial to protect themselves emotionally from pain they don't want to or are not ready to face. Because once they face or acknowledge the issue, they have to make a change, and change is always a challenge. Change can be scary. Change takes strength, courage, and dedication. A Queen of Denial doesn't want to deal. She wants the problem to go away on its own. And sometimes problems do go away on their own. Sometimes ignoring little things can be harmless. Sometimes it's wise to pick your battles and not dissect every single little thing that is not exactly perfect in a relationship. But sometimes being a Queen of Denial can be hazardous to your health.

For instance, if you are in a relationship with a man who has hit you and he convinces you he won't do it again, not only are you a Queen of Denial, you are putting yourself in a position to be physically hurt again. Or, if you are dating a man whom you think may be gay but you don't want to bring it up, embarrass him, or start an argument, not only are you a Queen of Denial, you are putting your health at risk. We all know how prevalent HIV is in the African-American community, and we also, unfortunately, know that there are a lot of brothers on the down low these days. If you see signs that your man may be gay or may be having sexual relations with someone besides you—a man or a woman—don't be in so much denial that you don't protect yourself. Don't be in so much denial that you put your own health at risk. Look at things for what they really are right now so you can save yourself a lot of future heartache, pain, and disappointment.

Another drawback to being a Queen of Denial is that it prolongs your point of no return. The longer you continue to lie to yourself, the longer you will put up with the problem and the longer it will take for you to walk away.

People who have been in a failed relationship (and that's everybody, isn't it?) can identify their point of no return. They may not have even known what it was when it happened, but once they look back they can pinpoint the exact moment when they knew the relationship was over. That doesn't mean it actually ended at that point, that moment, on that day. It just means that when it finally did end, they knew exactly when and why. And they may not have known exactly why right away, but once they really thought about it, it was clear.

A lot of times, women choose to ignore the point of no return and push forward in the relationship despite its occurrence. Most times, they regret it later. Most times, they wish they had acted on their innate knowledge, paid attention to their sixth sense and made a move. Unfortunately, many of us choose to stay, work it out, ignore the signs, and hold on—when there's nothing left to hold on to!

Not only is this detrimental to your relationship, it is detrimental to your self-esteem and your mental and physical health. When you know something is bad for you but you keep indulging in it, keep using things to suppress it, to drown out the voice of reason and consciousness, you make yourself sick. That's right. Staying in a sick relationship will make you sick, or worse, keep you sick. Because lying and untruthfulness, especially when it is internalized, just throws your whole energy system off. It just makes you wrong. You're just walking around, every day, lying to everybody and yourself, just being wrong. Wrongness is imbalance and imbalance can make you sick. In her classic book *You Can Heal Your Life,* Louise Hay addresses this phenomenon, saying: "I believe we create every so-called 'illness' in our body. The body, like everything else in life, is a mirror of our inner thoughts and beliefs. Continuous modes of thinking and speaking produce body behaviors and postures and 'eases' or diseases." So basically, if you keep lying to yourself you are going to make yourself sick. But this is not about being sick. It's about being whole and healthy. And if you are sick, it's about getting better. It's about healing yourself—body, mind, and spirit. It's all about recovering the right way from the wrong relationship.

So when you reach that point of no return, don't you dare deny it. Instead, face it, acknowledge it, and know that the point of no return may be the end of your relationship, but it is not the end of your life. The point of no return is really the beginning. The beginning of a journey toward the next phase of your life. At this point, the only way out is up.

NEWSFLASH: The point of no return will reveal itself as an "aha moment." You could be going along in your relationship with business as usual, and all of a sudden—bam!—you find yourself at your point of no return. You may have tried to ignore your relationship's short-comings in the past, but at this point, things can no longer be covered up, hidden, disguised, or denied. The point of no return can come as a shock to your system. But don't let it scare you or startle you. Recognize it for what it is—a wake-up call.

Chapter 2
READY? SET. LET HIM GO!

"Some people think it's holding on that makes one strong. Sometimes it's letting go." Sylvia Robinson

After everything I'd been through in my relationship— the pain, the clinging, the verbal abuse—I still remain in awe of women who choose to stay through much, much worse. I look at them intensely as I wonder why. I have asked myself this question and looked at the people and situations around me and have discovered some answers at the strangest times, in the most unexpected places.

Many years ago, I decided to take a legal proofreading course in an attempt to supplement my income. The course was taught by a smart, attractive young woman named Sherry. After the class, we chatted briefly, and although we'd just met, we, like women do sometimes, behaved as if we already knew each other and were simply picking up where we'd left off years, centuries, generations ago. While cracking jokes and sharing health tips, I noticed that although she had been doing legal proofreading for years, she had an artist's spirit. When I asked what she did besides proofreading, she was pleasantly surprised by my perceptiveness. Excited, she told me that, indeed, she was a filmmaker and was in the process of starting her own production company. She told me that she'd been doing the legal proofreading thing to finance her dream, and that she was finally set to open shop in a few weeks.

She was confident, focused, and driven, and I was sure she would succeed and wished her my best. A few months later, I called her at home to ask her some questions about a proofing problem I'd encountered. After she answered my questions, I inquired as to how her company was going. Sherry hesitated a moment, then told me that she'd had to put it on hold, that she'd had a few setbacks. I wanted to know if everything was fine, if she was all right, and she told me to watch *The Oprah Winfrey Show* at four, because she was going to be a guest and it would explain everything. So, of course, I made a point of tuning into *Oprah* that day, expecting to see Sherry talking about a tragic accident, an untimely death in her family, or how she was a victim of a nationwide real-estate scam. Basically, I was anticipating hearing about some disaster that would have hindered her from completing her clearly defined career goals.

That day, the show featured Dr. Phil, who was promoting his new book on making necessary changes in your life to ensure personal happiness. After explaining that he had ten steps that would be highlighted during the show, Oprah introduced her first guest, Sherry. Looking beautiful and stylish, Sherry read a letter she'd written to Oprah about how her boyfriend of two years had never introduced her to his parents despite her requests, how he never took her out, how he came over only at night and only at his convenience, and worse, how she always felt like she was being raped while they were having sex. Dr. Phil's advice to her was step number one, "Either you get it or you don't." He told her that she simply had to "get" that this man was not good for her and move on.

Now, at this point, I couldn't help but "get" it, too. This boyfriend, this relationship, was Sherry's disaster. Dealing with him and his neglect and emotional abuse had crippled her emotionally, stunted her so badly that she couldn't even move forward with her own best-laid plans.

A few days after the show aired, Sherry called me and asked if I'd seen the show. I told her I had and went on to inquire about what it was like meeting Oprah, the size of the hotel room, and the like. She told me she was treated like a queen, flown out to Chicago, had a limo waiting for her at the airport, and stayed in a luxury hotel suite. She said the highlight of the trip was, of course, meeting Oprah. Sherry told me that Oprah even pulled her aside after the show and told Sherry she could see her pain because she'd been in her shoes, but it was important that she leave the man. "As soon as you get home," Oprah told Sherry, "end the relationship." After hearing all of this, I couldn't resist, so I went ahead and asked Sherry if she'd ended it. "Well, um, not yet," Sherry told me as my mouth flew open in disbelief. Though I know how hard it was to decide to end my seven-year relationship, and I know there are many issues behind staying in a bad situation, I found it hard to believe that she hadn't ended the relationship, that she hadn't taken the ad-

vice of Oprah Winfrey, one of the most respected, successful women in the world. I found it hard to believe that
someone as smart and beautiful as Sherry wouldn't walk
away from a relationship that weakened her will to the point
where she was unable to get on with her life and pursue her
dreams.

In essence, that is the definition of a bad relationship.
Being unable to progress personally in a relationship with a
man is one of the main reasons to let him go. As women, we
are often sentimental about our men. We remember that
way we *used* to feel, how good it *was*, instead of looking at
how bad it *is*. Caught up in emotions, we become side-
tracked by unhealthy relationships and neglect our health
and careers. I've done it, and I've seen too many of my
friends do it, too: get so caught up in a man that they end up
sacrificing their careers, their livelihoods, their goals, their
dreams.

In my case, my ex was a very intelligent brother who was
always reading books and had many diverse and strong
opinions on various issues. At first, his brilliant mind and
intensity were extremely attractive in my eyes. I could sit
and listen to him talk for hours on end, but by the time I was
ready to formulate my own thoughts and voice my opinions,
he shot them down, picked them apart. Initially, I attributed
it to my belief that he was in fact smarter than I was. One
day, though, I remembered that although I am not a genius,
I am far from ignorant. Once we moved in together, he
began to stifle me creatively, which is a death sentence for a

writer. I like to think a lot; I like to talk a lot, too; but there are times when I simply space out. I like to just sit and think. Most times I think about nothing in particular, but sometimes I mentally play with my creative ideas, a story I'm working on, a character in a screenplay, etc. When I did this, he would criticize and tell me to stop spacing out, and when I tried to explain to him it was a part of my creative process, he told me I was just making excuses for wasting time. Again, I gave him the benefit of the doubt. I put his opinions before my personal truth and began to rationalize that maybe I was wasting time. Deep down inside, I knew this wasn't true. I knew that it was always in this state of being that I'd come up with and developed some of my best and most profitable ideas. I began to realize that he spaced out sometimes, too. The difference was that I respected him, and he didn't respect me. If I walked into a room and saw him in silent thought, I'd leave, get back to him later. If he came into a room where I was silent, he would begin talking loudly and urgently. It came to a point where I couldn't think straight, let alone write, and my writing suffered.

Some of you reading this may think that I'm being over-sensitive. *At least he wasn't hitting you or cheating on you*, you may be thinking. I agree. Being spiritually and cre-atively drained is nothing compared to being straight-up beat down. But whether problems in the relationship are trifling or tragic, we often rationalize them, make excuses, and stay. I knew six months into my relationship that he and I were not compatible. It took me seven years and a baby later to finally leave. Why? Why did I stay? Why do we stay? Why did Sherry stay even after Oprah Winfrey herself advised her to move on?

Fear! There are many other reasons, from financial to physical, from sexual to sinister, from the kids to the in-laws, from threats to treats. But the main reason behind it all is fear. As women—especially African-American women—we are continually hearing about how there are no good men out there. We become afraid to let go for fear that we won't find anyone else. We let supposed statistics sabotage us into staying.

Any decision in life made based on fear will be the wrong decision. First and foremost must come faith. Faith that you deserve better, faith that there is better, faith that the next time you will choose better.

As for me, it was extremely difficult to let go of the father of my child. We'd been together for seven years. And I needed him, right? Wrong. Once I realized this, I was able to let go of the relationship and get on with my life. It was scary, but I had to be strong. I knew that once he was gone, it would be on me, and it is. He still visits our daughter and is active in her development and education, but for the most part, it is on me. It is my shoulder she cries on, me who has to get up in the middle of the night if she can't sleep, me alone who does the food shopping, the cooking, and the cleaning. I make the decisions about where and how we live, and, ultimately, it is my emotions that rule me, no one else's. I won't lie; it would be nice to have someone around on a regular basis to share my life with, share the responsibilities.

I want that now and I wanted it then, but not enough to sacrifice my spirit. Indeed, it was my spirit that was suffering. I was tired all the time. Whereas I once was an optimistic dreamer, I became a cynical pessimist. I had to rescue myself. It was either him or me. I chose me. I loved him, but I chose to love me for a change. Although he claimed he loved me and says he still does, I had to listen to my inner voice, hear my spirit, and it wasn't at peace.

The thing is, he couldn't help it. He couldn't help who he was. I couldn't help who I was. Some people are not meant to be together. Some men, no matter what you choose to believe, are not the ones for you, and they simply cannot nurture you or give you what you need. Many times we are attracted to men because of their status, because of their brilliant minds, or just because they are straight up and simply fine. But we ignore the basics like energy. Some people tap your energy, and not all of them are men. There are the exasperating girlfriends, needy cousins, dependent coworkers; people who serve no real purpose in your life except to drain your energy. When your man is one of those people, he is not for you. He is your Mr. Wrong. One should feel invigorated and energized when being around a mate, not drained and continually misunderstood. There are other characteristics associated with men who might not be quite right for you no matter how hard you try or how long you have been together. Sometimes you and the man you are with are simply not compatible, and therefore he is a Mr. Wrong. But just because someone is a Mr. Wrong for you doesn't mean he is not someone else's Mr. Right.

There are deep-seated issues at hand that make the relationship, no matter how much love and commitment is there,
impossible to salvage. Characteristics of Mr. Wrong:

✦ He has a seriously scary temper. He gets mad really
easily, throws things, and kicks walls.

✦ He says things to you that shatter your self-esteem.
We all get angry and say things we shouldn't say to
one another in any relationship, but if you are continually being told bad things about yourself, it's not
healthy. Things like "Oh, that's why you didn't graduate medical school" or "I don't know why you are
even trying because you're never going to pass the
bar" are counterproductive and hurtful. You may realize he has a pattern of throwing things you tell him
about yourself back into your face during arguments
so the focus is taken off of him and his shortcomings.

✦ He makes you nervous. As in, walking on eggshells all
the time, afraid to do or say something that will set him
off and send him into a tailspin. This is no way to live.

✦ He is completely controlling. He doesn't want you to
keep in touch with family and friends. Your life is all
about him. This is due to his own insecurities, but it's
a dangerous place to be in because he is your sole
source of companionship and support. Creepy.

✦ He has crazy mood swings. One minute he's happy,
the next minute he's depressed. His life is a seesaw of
emotions, and you find yourself going through his unpredictable ups and downs.

✦ He disregards your feelings and opinions and makes you feel stupid. And worthless.

✦ He is a chronic cheater. I use the word "chronic" here because relationships have been known to survive infidelity. It's not impossible. But if it is something that you find yourself having to deal with over and over and over again, it's not worth it. You are risking your sanity and your health.

✦ He is a drug addict and/or an alcoholic. Basically, he is toxic. Toxic people are a danger to themselves and others. And in this case that means you. Toxic people pull you into their lifestyle. You may have been a casual drinker but find yourself drinking more and more. You may find your finances in jeopardy. You may find yourself arguing more often, especially after his frequent binges.

✦ He's "not sure" about the relationship or if you are "The One." This keeps you on an emotional roller coaster—up and down, back and forth—gives him way too much power, and makes you feel powerless.

✦ He doesn't love you fully and totally. No one wants "lopsided love," where he or she is the main person giving and cultivating the relationship on his or her own. There must be give-and-take. There must be balance.

Sometimes when we love someone, we make excuses for that person, or we try to "figure out" what his or her problem is. Sometimes it's simple, but sometimes it's not. According to Lundy Bancroft—author of *Why Does He Do That?*—there are countless reasons for a man's inappropriate behavior that really have nothing to do with you. They can be various and include:

He was abused as a child.

His previous partner hurt him.

He abuses those he loves the most.

He holds in his feelings too much.

He has an aggressive personality.

He loses control.

He is too angry.

He is mentally ill.

He hates women.

He is afraid of intimacy and abandonment.

He has low self-esteem.

His boss mistreats him.

He has poor skills in communication and conflict resolution.

He is a victim of racism.

He abuses alcohol, drugs, or engages in other addictive behavior.

Whatever the reason or reasons for his behavior, you have to know when to draw the line and recognize that unfortunately love is not enough. If you continue to be abused and mistreated, and your partner flat out refuses to change or get help, you have to walk away.

Leaving isn't always easy, though. Especially if, despite

this person's hindrances, you really do love him. Love doesn't ever end. But if you love someone who is self-destructive, who is unwilling to make real, concrete steps toward change, who ultimately doesn't love himself, or who doesn't, can't, or won't love you, you have two choices: stay and suffer or go and grow. That doesn't mean you have to, will, can, or should stop loving him. The heart has no limits. After all, God is love. Nevertheless, if your man exhibits habitual characteristics of Mr. Wrong, if he has issues, habits, even ideologies that you know that you, personally, cannot deal with, you have to let him go. For your own security. For your own sanity. You can't change a person who doesn't want to change, and you can't heal a person who doesn't want to be healed. Don't let guilt suck you into staying with someone whom you love but who mistreats you, disrespects you, doesn't appreciate you, or belittles you. Know that walking away is in fact an act of love: a love for you and a love for him. You can and you most likely will still always keep him in your heart. You can and you most likely will still care about him, be concerned for him, and hopefully pray for him. This does not mean that you should not do what is best for you and especially your children (if you have any) and get out. Walk away. Stop fighting. Let go.

In some circumstances, leaving and letting go is almost impossible. Especially if your finances are limited, or if he protests and refuses to leave or, worse, to let you leave. I was lucky because I rented the top floor in my grandmother's brownstone, so he had to move at my request because he knew my family was supporting my decision. But if we were renting an apartment somewhere else, or if the lease was in his name, it would have been much more complicated. Still, I would've found a way. If I had had to move and stay with my sister in Syracuse, or an old college buddy in Virginia, I would have, because it was that important to me. I could see and feel that I was being burdened by this man's presence in my life, and I wanted it to be over already.

Whatever your personal situation, once you have made the decision to move on, take the necessary steps. Make an "I'm Leaving Plan." Save your money, borrow from friends and/or family, and develop a support group that will be there for you through your transition. Talk to your children beforehand so you have their support also. Be prepared for them to become emotional and answer their questions and concerns with patience and understanding. It won't be easy; I know it's never easy to let go of a relationship, but when you know it's time, make your move.

Too often, the decision is already made for you. A man has ways of letting you know that he's not in love with you anymore or that he no longer cares about maintaining the relationship. It's not easy when you realize this, but once you do, it is up to you to make a change in your life: it is up to you to take control. You can ignore it or accept the reality and make the necessary adjustments. My college roommate always quoted the rapper Slick Rick when assessing relation- ships, saying, "Take hints quick and make the right change." Your eyes have to be open so you can see the hints. Some men are cowards, weak with words, and they won't tell you it's over: they'll show you. You must choose to see. Coming home late all the time (or not at all), insensitivity, callousness, neglect, and unprovoked verbal assaults are all signs that his interest in maintaining the relationship has waned. This type of behavior means he doesn't honor the relationship enough to try to make you happy.

My ex and I would have talks, discuss our problems and what changes we needed to make individually to continue to fortify our union. I would work on mine, such as talking on the phone. He said he disliked when I was on the phone with friends while he was home, so despite the stupidity and selfishness of the source of his displeasure, I made a point of staying off the phone when he was home. Unfortunately, he wouldn't even attempt to make personal changes that would please me. My peeve with him was that he yelled too much in front of our daughter. He didn't even try to change. In fact, he would start arguments deliberately to show me he didn't care about making me happy or saving our relationship. When we talked about it, he promised to try, but his actions spoke for themselves. Still, he would have stayed if I had been willing to let him get away with treating me any which way but right. He had a beautiful woman in his home when he got in at night, a beautiful daughter, a comfortable apartment, and somebody who was cooking for him and cleaning up after him. He wasn't going anywhere. If I hadn't made him move out, he would still be here, lying on me, tapping my energy, bringing me down.

One of the many things I learned from this experience is that if a man wants you and wants the relationship, you will know. If a man doesn't love you, is tired of you and the relationship, you will also know, simply by the way he treats you. Some men won't mistreat you intentionally. Some will come right out and tell you they want to end things. If you decide not to listen, decide to hold on and stick around, then they can get agitated, nasty, and end up mistreating you. Then things can get ugly and sad, which is why I believe that if a man says he wants to go, let him go. If he says it's not going to work, or he's a dog, or he's no good for you, believe him. It's painful but necessary so that you don't find yourself in a situation where you are being disrespected or mistreated.

We cannot change the way a person treats us, but we can change our reaction to the treatment. We can refuse to accept mistreatment by our actions, by walking away. This is hard if your senses are saying one thing and your emotions are saying another. As women we let our emotions rule us—we can't eat, can't sleep, can't think straight if the man we love isn't acting right. We need to grow up already! I remember once when I was a teenager, a boyfriend was supposed to call and he didn't. I moped around the house all evening, then finally whined to my mother, "Oh, why doesn't he just call me?" And my mother said, "And if he calls, then what? What will that mean for your life? How will that make your life better or more significant, or will it? Will it help you get into the college of your choice, or pass your finals?" I remember that every time I feel helpless about a man. After all, it really is quite ridiculous.

Getting control of our emotions is our challenge as women in relationships. We place way too much importance on the love and acceptance of men. If we learned to love our-selves, we wouldn't see young and old women walking around the streets half naked simply to attract male atten-tion. We wouldn't see women having baby after baby hoping to guarantee a man's love and loyalty. Of course, it is natural for us to want the love of men. We're human; we need love.

But some of the lengths women have gone through to get it are mind-boggling; some of the things women have done when they don't get it are downright sad. It's hard for us, I know, to put it all in perspective, but we must. I really be-lieve that it is actually our ultimate challenge to find a way, a balance where we allow ourselves to be the loving, nurtur-ing creatures we are without being so pathetically needy. The best way to avoid this is to be busy, stay busy, truly and honestly busy living your life, working on yourself, achiev-ing your goals and dreams, especially if you have a man in your life. That way you are genuinely occupied with your-self. That way *you* don't get lost. This doesn't mean that you can't cook for your mate, that you shouldn't be concerned with his wants and needs, but in order to not cross that line where your love for your man becomes clingy or overbear-ing, you should make every effort to become and stay inter-ested, active, and present in your own life.

As for men, their problem is control of themselves. They are not animals arbitrarily humping whatever female comes across their path with no regard for emotions or the results of their actions. They are men. God gave them the most su-perior brains of the kingdom so they can make choices with their heads and not their, well, heads. Anger, fear, fear of communication and commitment are all traits regularly associated with men, but the most common and painful for women is men's perceived inability to love just one of us at a time. Our main source of pain is their biggest challenge. Yes, there are so many of us and we are all so beautiful, it must be hard for them to choose, but choose they must, especially now with all the diseases going around and all the fatherless children in our community. It's really a matter of life and death. We can't tolerate anything less, and once we start to really stand our ground and are prepared to walk away from an unfaithful, insensitive man, we will see changes in our men. But we can be so emotional and needy that we'd rather put up with infidelity and insensitivity instead of being alone or moving on to the next relationship.

I know, I know. Not all men are cheaters. Some men can be monogamous, even prefer and embrace monogamy. I have been lucky and blessed enough to be in relationships where lack of fidelity was not the problem. And I am also aware that there are cultural differences surrounding this topic. A Muslim man and a Christian man are going to have different ideas, rules, and expectations regarding monogamy. And let's be real, women cheat, too. It's not about who does what. It's about us all working out the kinks individually so we can come together and experience happy, fulfilling relationships finally.

It obviously has to start with us. Men have work to do, too. Right now, though, I'm concerned with the work we, as women, have to do on ourselves. Men have to work it out among themselves if they are unhappy with the state of their relationships. All I know for sure is that as women we have to be willing to work on ourselves, love ourselves, so that we settle for nothing less than the best, and they, in turn, rise to the challenge. Nobody rises to low expectations.

When it comes to our relationships, African-American men and women are unfortunately deeply affected by so very many cultural and historical happenings that have created behavior that remains embedded in our psyche. It probably goes back as far as slavery, when Black people knew their loved ones could be killed or sold at any moment, on any given day. So we women were always fearful of losing our men. We tried our best not to rock the boat and to create a haven and make them comfortable under any and all circumstances. Though we are living in different times, Black men are still undeniably in danger of being wrongly accused by police; or being murdered in the street for no reason, like Amadou Diallo, Sean Bell, and so many others; or simply and sadly not making it back home at night. Compound that with the high unemployment and incarceration rates among Black men in America and you can see how we have become "understanding," "tolerant," and "devoted" due to these very real problems. The problem with this is sometimes some men do not deserve our devotion. Still we hang in there, make excuses and compromises. We end up paying the price for this kind of acquiescence, and sometimes it's the ultimate price. In her poignant book *Being a Strong Black Woman Can Get U Killed*, poet and women's activist Laini Mataka addresses this issue when she writes "She [the Strong Black Woman] died from tolerating Mr.

Pitiful just to have a man around the house." When I recently read this poem, I was struck by how much it rang true for so many women I know who, despite living in the twentieth century, are holding on to unfulfilling relationships with unevolved men as if the lynch mob will be riding up on horses at any given moment, women who are happy to be able to boast, "I have a man" despite the circumstances surrounding this "achievement."

Case in point: a young woman who has a two-year-old daughter and is married to a Navy man. Though they were never serious and he told her he didn't love her, she ended up pregnant by him and he offered to marry her so their child could receive benefits from the Navy. So they were married, though they rarely saw each other, and when they did, they would argue and fight. He would call her fat and stupid and would criticize the way she cared for the baby. He even hit her when he felt so inclined. To top it off, although he claimed he married her so she and their baby could benefit from his Navy status, the money he received that was supposed to be allotted to his wife and child was used for payments on a new car. He gave her $100 a month, while she and her daughter lived with her aunt and sister in a crowded, cluttered apartment. He did not care if she or even their child was uncomfortable and unhappy. All he cared about was his monthly car payments. When she threatened to tell the authorities about his actions, he threatened her with physical violence. He then promised to give her the money for an apartment after he finished paying off the car note. So she stayed. Though she was miserable and would rarely hear from him while he was away—no sweet calls to say "I love you" for this sister—she stayed married to him. She even admitted to me that she liked the way people looked when she told them she was married, and she loved the diamond wedding ring on her finger. But most of all she had a man. Under whatever circumstances, she had a man. Her entire family has spoken to her about the danger and unfairness of this situation and assured her she will have their utmost support if and when she decides to end the marriage, but she is convinced that despite the fact that he is a fraud and a wife beater, they can make it work! She is young, only twenty-one, and hopefully she will wise up and get out of the relationship so she can began building a better life for herself and her daughter.

But when it comes to staying with a bad, basically useless man, age ain't nothing but a number. When I was contemplating ending my relationship, I went to a family friend who is like an aunt to me, who lived with her fifteen-year-old son's father. After telling her about my situation, how my mate was verbally abusive, drank too much, spent too much money, was callous, immature, and insensitive, she told me to hang in there. She told me it's not that bad, and I should try to make it work for my daughter. Mind you, this is the same woman whose son's father left the country when their son was born only to return eight years later jobless. She welcomed him with open arms and has been taking care of him ever since, all because she believes her son needs a man around the house. But the son and the father fight all the time, each childishly vying for her attention. As a result, this once vibrant and voluptuous woman has become thin and drawn. In addition, since he's been back, she's been smoking cigarettes, and it shows in her black lips and watery eyes.

As she spoke to me, giving me what I'm sure she thought was good advice, I took a good look at her. I remembered all the complaining she used to do about how he never helped around the house. The complaining had stopped years before, when she kept getting the same response from her sisters and friends: "So why don't you end it?" Maybe she knew the answer to that question but didn't want to share it, but obviously, she chose not to end the relationship for whatever reason. She was a grown woman, and we had to respect her choice to stay in the relationship although it was painful to watch. I even had to wonder why I had gone to her for advice in the first place when I knew she wasn't happy and probably couldn't give me the best advice due to her state of mind, but I guess I just needed to talk to someone and she was there. If I had been more strategic, I would have gone to someone who was more qualified to answer my questions and address my concerns from a positive perspective and a place of power. Still, although her advice wasn't the best, I'm glad I talked to her because hearing her tell me to put up with all I was dealing with was so ludicrous that it was like a trigger for me.

Suddenly, being alone wasn't such a scary thought. Suddenly I knew it was more important for me to be strong and sane than in a relationship. I realized that there are worse things that could happen to me than being a single mother. I admitted that I did want it all—the man, children, career, healthy body, strong mind, and sincere spirit—and I acknowledged that I could have it all, but not with him. He was just one of the components, and I could still have all those other things without him. Maybe one day I would meet someone who was more compatible, who wasn't always badgering me. I didn't know about that. I just knew I had to be able to think straight, hear my own inner voice, tap into my God-given talents, and that I couldn't do those things with this particular person in my life.

Real love is sometimes tough love. We have to be stronger so men can be stronger. If they knew they couldn't get away with certain things, they wouldn't do them. Women often complain about men being insensitive and/or unwilling and unable to talk, open up. Believe me, if they knew they had to find a way to communicate their feelings before they could spend any time with you, they would find a way, whether it be through counseling, or seeking out a mentor, or talking to a reverend. Women do have the power. We are in control. Unfortunately, we fail to realize this. We think that we have to tolerate unacceptable behavior. But it has to stop! For our daughters' sakes, we can no longer remain in relationships because we are afraid to be alone. For our sons' sake, we have to show them that there are real responsibilities that come with being a man and that disrespecting women will not be tolerated. Think of the future. We do not want our children to be faced with the same problems we have, but they will if they grow up in households where daddy goes out all night but mommy wakes up and pretends everything's okay, or worse, reciprocates with spending the night out herself. Children see us, and we have to decide if what they are seeing is appropriate. I think maybe if I hadn't had a child, I would've been more tolerant of my boyfriend's behavior. Maybe it wouldn't have upset me so much when he would rant and rave around the house, cursing me out. But my daughter was watching. She was eighteen months old, but she knew what was going on. Once after an argument, he stormed out of the bedroom and I fell onto the bed sobbing; my daughter toddled over to me and patted me on the back. The feeling of that sweet, small hand gave me the strength to let go. What was I going to do, have her see me get cursed out and disrespected in the day, then lying in the bed with him at night? Is that what I wanted for her future? No, it wasn't.

So my decision was a clear one, based on my truths. Your decision must be based on your own truths. One universal truth is that some relationships are not meant to last forever. Some people are lessons. Before I met my ex, I did not have the extensive knowledge of the healing powers of herbs that I do now, which I learned from him, nor did I have my funny, talented, beautiful little girl. So I am thankful. I am most thankful, though, that I had the wisdom and strength to see that we were finished. We'd taught each other all there was to teach each other. It was over.

As women, we are particularly prone to holding on to things when it is time to let them go—be it a man, a job, or a way-too-small pair of shoes. Because one day, your feet are going to miraculously fit into those shoes, right? Well, maybe if you lose some weight they might fit a little better—this is true. But if you're a size twelve, no amount of weight loss is going to get you into a size eight. But you try anyway—they were on sale; you had to have them; they go with everything. But every time you wore them, you experienced excruciating pain, mind-numbing discomfort. Finally, you gave up and found yourself a pair of shoes that fit. The lesson learned? If it don't fit, don't force it!

Things coming to an end and changing is a part of nature. Just as there are evergreen trees, some relationships last forever and stand the test of time. But some are not meant to be that way. They bloom and then die. Acknowledge the change, mourn the death, and move on. You have nothing to lose, and what you gain is a more fulfilled life and a chance for a better relationship the next time around. So no matter how hard you think it will be, at some point you have to get yourself, your mind-set, and your life Ready, Set, and Let Him GO!

Relationship Levels

Most likely, the longer the relationship lasted, the harder it was to let go. Take a moment to look at the levels that follow and decide if yours was a Level One, Level Two, or Level Three relationship.

Level One: This was a short-term relationship of eight months or less (usually less). You two were just dating and may have been seeing other people. Maybe it was a summer fling or an affair, but both parties knew that it was not going to be long term, or at least there were no real commitments made. This person was nice to be around but wasn't around all the time. You probably dated a few weekends out of each month and enjoyed movies or dinners together. He was a companion. The intention was to get to know one another better and see where the relationship could go. There was not much invested in this relationship (emotionally, financially, etc.). There may or may not have been sexual intimacy.

Level Two: This relationship probably lasted a little over six months to a few years, during which time you and this person became very close. There were definite loving feelings, and words of love were most likely exchanged. Things were hopeful and looking good. You two spent a lot of time together and were becoming more and more a part of each other's lives. There was an unspoken or spoken commitment. There was physical and/or emotional intimacy with this person.

Level Three: This was a long-term relationship, and there was a clear commitment made—either marriage, engagement, or cohabiting. This person was a permanent part of your life for a long time. Both parties at some point in the relationship expressed words of love. There was a significant investment of time, emotions, finances, and more.

Obviously, a man from a short-term relationship who wasn't in your life for long may be easier to let go of than a man from a long-term, committed relationship and especially from a marriage. It depends on how much you love the person, how much you want the relationship to work, how many compromises are made by both parties. Sometimes a short-term (Level One) relationship can be harder to let go of than a longer relationship because sometimes shorter is sweeter and the end can be a disappointment or a surprise, whereas with a long-term (Level Three) relationship, there is enough time for anger and bitterness to grow and ugly sides to show, so when it's over, it could be a relief. But if it's a short-term relationship you are having a hard time letting go of, look on the bright side. You've invested only a few months—not years—in the relationship. It has been an inexpensive experience. Some experiences in life you pay a lot for, and in relationships we pay the price with time and energy. In the case of a long-term relationship, think of all the time and energy you have already put into it and don't waste a bit more. Regardless of whether this person was a part of your life for a long or short time, however, you did have a connection with this person, so it will be hard, you will hurt, and you should mourn the relationship in one way or another.

So far our discussion, for the most part, has taken place under the assumption that it was you who decided to (or will) walk away no matter how difficult or for whatever reason. Even if it was something you wished you didn't have to do, you did it anyway, and it's empowering when you make any decisions or take any actions that are based on your own needs and well-being. On the contrary, what about when it is you who has been left? What about if it was a relationship that you cherished, that you were happy in, but the other person chose not to continue the relationship? Maybe he just wasn't happy, maybe he got scared, maybe he's seeing someone else or wants to see other people, or maybe he feels you are Ms. Wrong for him. How do you handle that? That is where the real emotional challenge comes in, because despite how much you love the person, you cannot make someone love you back. You can't force someone to stay if he has already decided to go. This is the more painful of the two scenarios because when it is you who walks away, you feel empowered, but when it is the other person who walks away, you feel powerless. Your ego is bruised. You are confused, and self-doubt ensues. When you walk away, it is you who is doing the heart breaking; when he walks away, it is your heart that is being broken.

Still, you have to let go. Try to do it with some decorum and pride. You can state how you feel, how you wish things were; you can express your love and disappointment; but you don't have to beg, break things, spit, and curse! Instead, take a deep breath, get a grip on your emotions, and remember your self-worth. Remember that you should never have to beg or plead for someone to be with you, to stay with you. Emotions are unpredictable, and you never know what you will do when faced with a painful situation. And it's all right to be emotional, but once it's all over and said and done, once you've done all your kicking and screaming only to realize he really is walking out the door, you can and will be addressing some hard questions about yourself so that you don't find yourself in the situation again. Not to say that your heart won't ever be broken again, that a man won't walk away again—love is all about taking chances, making a gamble and seeing where the chips fall. I wish I could tell you differently. I wish I could tell you that self-examination, growth, and self-acceptance will guarantee that you won't have future relationship challenges, that you won't have your heart broken by a man ever again. I cannot. What I can tell you is that the odds of this happening will be much less because you are clear about what you want and don't want, what you can handle and what you cannot. You will no longer be afraid of losing anyone once you have a true hold on yourself and are truly self content.

Friends with Your Ex: To Be or Not to Be?

That is the question that comes up over and over again once a relationship ends. When I brought the topic up on my blog, hesgoneyoureback.blogspot.com, and was confronted with women who had so many different opinions, I realized it's a really personal, really individual decision. Some women responded that some of their very best friends are exes, that just because the relationship didn't work out does not mean that the friendship and bond formed has to be discarded, too. But other women said they would never consider it, that once a man is out of their lives, he is out for good. It ultimately is a personal decision. For me, I have an ex-boyfriend from high school whom I talk to all the time. I give him child-rearing advice and tips on how to shop for his wife. We have known each other for so long it would be pointless to stop being platonic friends with him. The real reason why I can be friends with this person, besides the fact that we went together so long ago, is that I was never really in love with him. I never envisioned sharing my life with him or having him be that person for me. So I have no animosity or jealousy toward his family. I am happy for him. I am unfazed. But in the case of the boyfriend who cheated on me, I have nothing to say to him. Ever. Why would I? Then there was another guy whom I really wanted to and tried to be friends with. We went out a few times after we broke up and stayed in touch, but then I had to admit to myself that I wasn't comfortable with the situation, I still had love for him, I wasn't that detached, and it was best to remove him from my life completely. On the other hand, I was dating a man for a few months who had become a good friend. We talked a lot and we liked to go out together. I thought I was making a friend, but once I realized he had romantic interests and I did not, the friendship kinda fizzled. Which was for the best, because he wasn't really a friend—he was a love interest. I just wasn't interested.

So when deciding whether or not to be friends with your ex, you have to define what a friend is to you. To me, a friend is someone who loves you unconditionally, truly wants the best for you, and genuinely supports you in your quest for lifelong happiness and fulfillment. Is the guy you broke up with because you were dissatisfied with the relationship really that person? Is the guy who broke up with you because he wasn't happy really that person? Maybe so. Maybe not. But only you can make that decision.

So I guess it's a personal decision that depends on your personal situation. If the relationship ended on bad terms— if there was a lot of fighting, crying, and cursing—being friends will probably not be an option. Both parties are most likely through with each other anyway, because there was such bitterness and animosity in the relationship that being friends is not even an option. But in some situations, where the breakup was mutually agreed upon or was ended without any fanfare, people find that they can remain friends. This is really rare, though, because feelings are still raw and sometimes you or the other person may agree to stay friends in hopes of eventually reconciling the relationship. This is where things become tricky and sticky, because someone is going to move on first, and if it's not you, can you really handle it? If you are sure you can, then by all means stay friends. If this is a person you love and trust and just couldn't make it in a relationship with, by all means keep him in your life if you wish. Just be sure that you are doing so for the right reasons and that you or he doesn't have any latent feelings—they can jump up and bite you in the you know what!!! You basically have to know what you are capable of. If you are open-minded and have really let go, feel free to go for it! Be friends. I've known people who have introduced their exes to their friends, who have invited their exes to their weddings and vice versa, and who actually hang out with and talk to their exes on a regular basis. But if it was a diffi-cult relationship, it's probably best to cut all ties so you can really heal.

I have found that in general being friends with an ex is not such a good idea despite the best of intentions, espe-cially immediately after you've broken up. I've discovered through trial and error that to really let go you have to really let go. No phone calls. No e-mails. No texts. No blog com-ments. Nothing. Especially if this was a Level Three relation-ship. It may take some time to get used to not having that other person around, or seeing him regularly, or speaking with him a lot. But if you don't get used to it once and for all, you might find yourself using the "friendship" as a crutch for companionship. Maybe, eventually, after you have settled into your life without him, you can be cordial and send Christmas cards and birthday wishes, but for now, step back and get yourself acclimated to life without that person.

Of course, if children resulted from the relationship, there will need to be some sort of communication. Just make it cordial and keep it short and sweet in the beginning. Re-member the breakup is painful for the children, too. This is the only instance where I think it's advisable to try to be friends with your ex so that eventually you can spend time with the kids together. Again, it's all relative. Just use your best judgment: be sure there are no ulterior motives, under-lying resentments, or unresolved issues between you. Only you can decide if your ex is really friendship material.

Suffer All the Little Children

Breakups are hard on everyone involved, and if you have children, they are involved. They see you hurt, angry, and confused, and they don't know what in the world is going on! It's your job to navigate them through this hard time. It won't be easy. You have your own issues, your own wounds to lick. Still, as a mother, it's your job to support your children through times of challenge and change.

Everyone's situation is different. The dynamics of each individual family are unique. But if this was a Level One relationship—someone you have been dating briefly—most likely your children haven't become attached. Maybe they haven't even met him, which is all the better. But if they have met him and you know he won't be coming around anymore, be honest. Tell them that you two were spending time together to see if you wanted to go forward with the friendship and have decided that you do not.

But if it was a serious, long-term, Level Three relationship, the transition will be more challenging for them, specifically if the breakup was with their father. You have to let them mourn the loss of the relationship, too. If you know that their father will still remain in their lives despite the split, reassure them of this. Tell them that it will take a little time to adjust to the change and to figure out exactly how and when they will see and spend time with their dad. Ask them to be patient, understanding, and supportive, and you might be pleasantly surprised at their response.

But if you know that they won't be seeing much of daddy from now on for whatever reason, you should probably be honest about this, too, no matter how hard it will be.

If the breakup was not with their father but instead with someone you were married to, a stepfather, or lived with, then young children will surely be affected. They were used to having this person around the house, just like you were. Maybe they formed a bond with him, or maybe they didn't even like him. Regardless, it's a big change for all involved, and children's feelings should not be ignored or denied. Ideally, if you and your ex are willing and able to sit down with the children together and explain the situation, this would be great. The children will see that it's a unified decision and may be reassured that just because the relationship with you is over does not mean the relationship with them is over. Some men still may want to see the kids—even if they are not their biological kids. You two should discuss this before you meet with the children.

But if it's a different situation, consider the children may be heartbroken, too. Explain to the children why he left or why you asked him to leave. Of course you don't have to give all the dirty details, but be as honest as you can. He was disrespectful. I was unhappy. Whatever the reason is, be clear but try your best not to use words of anger or to curse or to call him names. Let them see you handle the situation with dignity and grace at all times.

Once the relationship is really over and you and your children are on your own, make sure you don't become alienated from one another. No matter how much you may want to, don't retreat into a shell. Don't be inaccessible to your children. Make an extra effort to spend time with them. The best way to do this for now is to do what they like to do. Now is not the time to drag them to a museum and introduce them to Renaissance art or African sculpture—unless they are already interested in that type of thing. No. Now is the time to suck it up and play the video game. Now is the time to compromise and watch that horror movie or sit through the football game. Because it's really not about what you are doing. It's about being together. Think about creating new habits and rituals that have nothing to do with the guy who is long gone.

Try dating your children. Yes! Seriously. Take *them* out to dinner or to see a movie or a play. Make every Friday or Saturday night an event. Let everyone get dressed up and go somewhere special and do something different. Expose them to culture, music, and the arts. Once my agent informed me that she had two tickets available for an Aretha Franklin concert and asked me if I wanted them. I said yes, of course, and decided to take my daughter with me. We went together and of course had a wonderful time. More importantly, my daughter—who, like the rest of her peers, is so used to young starlets who can't sing shaking and shimmying all over the place to disguise the absence of any real talent—had the opportunity to witness a legend like Aretha Franklin stand in one spot in a beautiful gown and saaang! Live. It was my first time seeing her live myself, and although I've heard her records and have seen her perform on television, I must say that none of that did her justice. To really appreciate the uniqueness and beauty of her voice, you have to hear it live. Anyway, so there we were, my daughter and I, jamming to Aretha Franklin at New York's Radio City Music Hall on a Friday night. I looked over at her and was so glad she was there with me and was so glad I decided to bring her instead of the guy I was dating at the time. I was so glad I chose to spend this particular Friday night with my child.

You don't have to always go out to have quality time with your children. If you have girls, have a beauty night with them, not your girlfriends. Do each other's toes, give each other facials. You will be bonding with your young ladies while teaching them invaluable beauty, grooming, and self-care tips. Or maybe even go to a spa together or have concurrent hair appointments.

As for boys, they might take the breakup hard and not even show it. They might not want to admit they are hurt. They might not know how to say they are angry. Most likely, if you look, there will be signs. They might get into trouble at school or stop doing homework. But you have to spend time with them to see the signs. If your boy has bonded with the man, you might want to make sure he spends time with males you love and trust, like your brother or your uncle, your dad or your best male friend. If you don't have anyone at your disposal, look into getting him a male mentor. Just do your best to ensure he has someone from the same sex to relate to and share his feelings with. Ultimately, though, if your child—boy or girl—is having an uncharacteristically hard time dealing with the breakup, if you see there are some real emotional issues developing, don't hesitate to seek professional help. Children can and do benefit from therapy and counseling.

When it comes to kids, never underestimate the power of a good, old-fashioned distraction. Get those girls into dance class. Put that boy in basketball camp. Or vice versa, depending on their abilities and interests. This way you will have time to take care of yourself sometimes. If new activities for the kids are not feasible financially, try to find free programs or after-school activities. If you still are unable to get them into any programs, find something for them to do around the house. Depending on their age, they can do little projects like folding clothes or organizing magazines. Reward them for cleaning their rooms or cleaning the mirrors. Give them an age-appropriate household chore. Just try your best to keep them as busy as possible.

When you decide to let go of a relationship, it is a decision you and only you can make. But if children are a part of the equation, it's best to be sensitive to the reality that their lives are being overhauled, too. So be patient with them. Play with them. Pray with them. Talk to them. Teach them how to cook. Spend time in the kitchen creating a feast or just an afternoon snack. Experiment with different recipes or show them how you make their favorite dish. Letting the kids help you out in the kitchen can be real fun as long as you all are careful. Kids like to be helpful; it makes them feel important, necessary, needed. So let them help you out in the kitchen. Depending on their age, kids can add ingredients, stir cake batter, and of course are always helpful when it comes to licking the spoon! Another good way to bond with children, while having fun and creating something, is to do arts and crafts projects. You can have them cut out certain words or letters from magazines for a collage, or you can let them glue macaroni or beans onto a container to make a decorative vase. My daughter and I like to go through our old photo albums, find pictures of ourselves or of friends and family members whom we like, then make copies of them on our computer's printer and put together great, wonderful photo collages. That's our thing, but there are so many other creative things to do with your children. Comedienne and former talk-show host Rosie O'Donnell recently wrote a great book called *Crafty U* that has great ideas and simple instructions for doing arts and crafts projects with kids. They can make picture frames, cutouts, and all kinds of great stuff. But it's really about doing something fun and creative together. As Rosie says, "Make a memory."

Children grow up fast. Never forget that once they grow up and get out of the house, things will never be quite the same. Utilize this unfortunate, sad time when you're going through a breakup to fortify your relationships with your children. Your children can be your greatest source of love, support, strength, and inspiration, if only you will let them. Don't shun them or turn them away because you are suffering. Allow them to help you heal. On non–school nights, allow them to cuddle with you under the covers, on your big fluffy pillows, while watching an age-appropriate movie, reading to you from their favorite book, or just talking to you about what's going on with their lives and their friends at school. Soon, with a little patience and creativity, every-thing will be running smoothly. You and your children will just need a little time.

Anger Management

When we find ourselves in situations that are challeng-ing and unexpected, we get mad. It's okay to be mad. It's understandable to be angry. You're hurt. Being hurt doesn't give you an excuse to be hurtful. Just because you're going through what you're going through, you don't have an ex-cuse to snap at people, yell at your kids, or blow up at your friends. It's especially not fair to young children, because they are helpless and at your mercy. They really can't do anything about mommy's mood swings or bouts of anger.

On the other hand, your friends or adult family members just might snap right back at you and put you in your place. For your sake, I hope they do. I hope you get stinky and abra-sive and short-tempered with one of your real good friends so they can tell you off real good. So they can let you know how ugly you are being. So they can snap you back into real-ity and force you to face your feelings of frustration and dis-appointment. Controlling your anger and turning all that negative energy into something positive is a real challenge. But you can do it. You can and should take a deep breath be-fore you open your mouth. You can and should take a nap if you are feeling overwhelmed. You can and should take a walk if you are feeling edgy and restless. You can and should make a conscious effort to be loving and kind to the people who love you, regardless of what you're going through. What's your other option? Walking around being a shrew and wondering why no one—man, woman, or child—wants to be bothered with you? This transition is not going to be easy. Some days you will get tired. Some days you will be sad. Most days you will be mad—just don't become maniacal. Make the transition easy for all involved by handling this test of strength like a woman who is in control, like a woman who is a queen.

Money Matters

Despite all of your emotional turmoil and familial upheaval, there is one last thing that you must manage, must not drop the ball on, must not neglect, must not adopt the attitude of "it will work itself out," because when it comes to this, it won't. What am I referring to? If you don't already know, I'm talking about the green, bread, dough, paper. Yes, ladies, I'm talking about money. No matter the circumstances behind your relationship, you still have to eat. No matter how much you hurt him, you still have bills to pay. No matter how much he hurt you, the kids still need school tuition, new clothes, and regular doctor visits. Granted, if you were in a Level One or Level Two relationship, money will probably not be a big issue because you two most likely didn't have any or many monetary entanglements. But if you did, or if this was a Level Three relationship, if you were living together or even married, splitting the pot is not going to be easy, so don't expect it to be. More important, don't expect anyone involved to have your best interests at heart. If someone does, good for you. Just don't count on it. Count on yourself to make sure your situation is straight. If leaving or letting go means canceling your bank accounts, transferring funds, moving mortgages, do what you have to do for you. Make sure no one has access to your credit cards or bank accounts but you.

Thankfully, many of us are smart and savvy when it comes to money management. Unfortunately, many of us are not. Many of us have left the money handling to the men. If that is you, don't feel bad. According to female financial guru Suze Orman, this phenomenon is ingrained in us and is nothing new. Nor is it exclusive to Black women. According to Ms. Orman, it affects all women. In her long-overdue book *Women & Money*, she prods readers to consider that women tend to nurture others as a basic instinct but we do not generally take care of our finances like we do our partners, our kids, or even our plants. Our relationship with our money is dysfunctional. But unlike dysfunctional love relationships, we cannot walk away from our relationship with money. We have to get it right. It's something that must be addressed and handled in order for us to survive. But if you are wondering how to repair your relationship with money, Ms. Orman has the answer for you: "The same way you would repair any relationship that is damaged: by acknowledging your mistakes, taking responsibility, and resolving to act in a way that will bring about change for the better."

So you see, it's not hopeless. There is something you can do. Right now! Go and get yourself a piece of paper and a pen. Write down a list of ALL your expenses. Your housing expenses. Transportation. Food. Clothes (don't be shy). Doctor's visits for you and/or the kids. Everything. Every little thing you spend money on regularly. Now, after that honest purge of information, write down how much money you make, how much money you have on hand, how much money you have in the bank, all of that. You can include investments and retirement funds, mutual funds, and 401(k) plans, but for now focus on what is liquid—what you can put your hands on today, right now—and work with that number. At this point don't worry about what you will or won't get in the divorce settlement or whether or not your ex will have some integrity and go ahead and give you back the money you lent him to fix his car last month or whether you will get help from a friend or family member. If everything adds up well, then kudos to you—just make sure that with your new situation, you can maintain.

All of this is scary, I know. No one to split the bills with. No one paying that cell phone bill for you. No one to fall back on. No one but you. And your money. And your money management skills. And you and only you know how good or bad those skills are. Assess them honestly to determine if you will indeed need help from an outside source like a financial planner or an accountant. If that is the case, don't be afraid or embarrassed to seek help if you can find it and afford it. If you can't, this might be a project you have to embark upon on your own. It can seem scary, but it's really an opportunity for you to learn how to manage your money, once and for all, so that despite the state of your love life your money is right.

In her book, Ms. Orman also cautions that with a divorce rate at 40 percent, a lot of women will find themselves handling their money solo. The same goes for women who marry later in life, never marry, or are single parents. She reminds us that many women fail to really deal with their money matters until they are forced to, until they have no choice. Well, right now you have no choice. You have to own up to your strengths and weaknesses and face your finances. This isn't going to be easy. This is surely going to be a challenge. Especially if you are one of the many women who, after the end of a long relationship, find themselves "feeling divorced but never married" because although they lived with or were taken care of by their mate for years, they have no real claim to anything because they never married for whatever reasons. They have no legal safety net and need to divest their finances to avoid poverty. Women specifically in this situation need to take action immediately.

Whatever your situation, look at it, assess it, and address it. Now. If you know you need to get a job, start looking. Now. Do you know your credit score? Do you have life insurance? Home insurance? Apartment renters' insurance?

Car insurance? Do you have an IRA? Any mutual funds? A 401(k) plan? Do you know what these are? How they work? Why they are important, even imperative?

Many women were never really taught anything about money management. This is especially true of Black women, many of whom grew up in households where talking about money was considered rude or crass, where money was discussed between adults and behind closed doors, where the average household income was markedly less than that of a white family, where our history of struggle and scraping to get by had ingrained in us a mentality of lack instead of one of prosperity. We know the basics: save more, spend less. Pay your bills on time. Balance your checkbook. Use cash instead of credit whenever possible. But we are not taught about how money grows, how to make our money work for us. If you took economics in high school or college, consider yourself lucky, but still it's not the same as growing up in an environment where money was discussed openly and honestly, where investments were family decisions, where watching the stock market was a daily activity. In high school I remember clearly how, during lunchtime, the Black kids would be at one table playing spades and the white kids would be at the other reading the *New York Times*, glued to the stock-market section. At the time, I thought they were just crazy and corny. At the time, I knew nothing about how the stock market works. At the time, I thought nothing of the fact that all of my Black friends always had the latest designer styles and jeans and sneakers— no matter how much they cost, regardless of whether they could really afford it. Now I see that this too is detrimental to our culture. We love to look good, but what do our bank accounts look like?

Overall, I believe women haven't been taught much about money because money is power and to be ignorant about money is to be powerless. I believe the same holds true for Black folks. What better way to keep a group of people oppressed than to keep them financially illiterate? Of course, at this point, that's no excuse. There is information out there for the taking. There is power waiting to be claimed. Now is the time to go forth fearlessly, my sister friends, and claim it!

NEWSFLASH: The moment you are really ready to go, he's going to do something to make you want to stay. That's right, the same man who treated you with indifference, wouldn't change, couldn't compromise, didn't hear your pleas before will now do something, say something, or buy you something to convince you that things can change, that things can get better. And you know what? They can change, and maybe they will. But you still have to go. If you were in so much pain and despair that you went through all the trouble to pack your stuff, make arrangements to stay somewhere else, and do all the other things that a move like this entails, then don't let anything or anyone stop you now. Stay focused. He won't be able to believe you're actually doing it; you're actually going to go. He may not take it very well, and that's where it's up to you to know your man. If he has a history of violence, you might want to bounce under cover of night or have someone there with you when you are leaving. Just be prepared. Leaving is not going to be easy. No one wants to admit failure, especially not a prideful man, especially not when it comes to his woman. If you're lucky, you won't have to go through any of this. If you're lucky, your transition will be a smooth one, with no one blocking you. If you're lucky, your man will handle your leaving in a mature and levelheaded way. If you're smart, you'll hope for the best and expect the worst.

Chapter 3

AVOID THE ABYSS

"The price of hating others is loving oneself less."
Eldridge Cleaver

It is so cold here. And dark. It's kind of scary, too. It's the Abyss, and it is a place you don't want to be. Because once you go there, it is extremely difficult to pull yourself out of it. *What exactly is the Abyss?* you ask. I define the postrelationship abyss as a mental state of darkness and despair that can lead to depression and desperation. When experiencing any type of loss, there are countless emotions and states of mind, or stages, that one can experience. The most common five stages are denial, anger, bargaining, depression, and acceptance. With denial, you basically refuse to let your mind accept that the relationship is really over. Maybe you still wear your wedding ring or haven't even told anybody about the breakup yet. Maybe you still haven't unsubscribed to that wedding Web site. Maybe you keep his clothes in the closet, refuse to remove his key from your chain, and possibly pretend that the relationship didn't end at all, that you two will reconcile any minute now.

As for the anger stage, you are just damn mad. Mad at

the situation, mad at your ex, mad at yourself. Mad at what was said. Mad at what was left unsaid. Angry as hell about the turn of events, about the way things went down. And pissed way off—especially after all you put up with and sacrificed!

When you hit the bargaining stage, you are ready to do anything to salvage the relationship, to work things out. You figure if he could only change "A" about himself, and you could only change "B" about yourself, the relationship would be salvageable. You convince yourself that the big problem—whatever it was, whomever it was—is not so big after all, that you can indeed tolerate it, that he can indeed accept your shortcomings. In this stage you may make a call or accept a call or do something to be able to see him so you two can "talk about the relationship" even though you both know everything has already been said and done.

Depression, well. You know. A lot of crying, a lot of self-pity, a lot of sleeping. You're not hungry. You're always tired. You don't want to go on. You're, you know, depressed. The thing about depression is that it can be extremely dangerous if not dealt with, acknowledged, and fought like the evil beast that it is. Depression can rob you of your energy, your ambition, your simple will to go forward. And the longer it lasts, the worse it gets. The longer you let it linger, the longer you will lie around feeling sorry for yourself, being sad and depressed. In her book *Can I Get a Witness?: Black Women and Depression*, Julia Boyd acknowledges that postbreakup depression is extremely common in women for various reasons. "Women tend to view themselves as failures when a relationship doesn't work out," she indicates and goes on to provide a few important facts about depression: "Depression is more than sadness or the blues; Depression is known clinically as a mood disorder; Depression is treatable."

Then, thankfully, comes acceptance. You finally get it. You finally face it. You are able to look the situation square in the face and yourself straight in the eye and acknowledge it: the relationship is over. For real and for good. Acceptance is actually a beautiful, blessed, merciful state to find yourself in, because once you can acknowledge a situation and accept it, you can move on.

As for the aforementioned Abyss, it happens somewhere after the anger stage of recovery. The thing is, anger is inevitable, but the Abyss is avoidable.

Regardless of the circumstances behind your relationship's end, there are the normal feelings of pain and confusion. If he left you, the pain will probably be worse, leading to questions like "What did I do wrong?" If you were the one to leave him, you'll find that when you're lonely and alone you ask yourself, "Did I do the right thing?" Either way, the relationship has ended, and whether you like it or not, there has been a change in your life. And change is always challenging. Change is never easy.

The feelings you experience at this time are yours to embrace. Even the anger at your ex *and* yourself is to be expected. But it is how you choose to navigate these feelings that matters. Your main course of action, though, needs to be actively and consciously avoiding the Abyss.

How do you know when you're headed straight to the dreaded place? Hmm. Let's see. When you're ready to call him and curse him out for the twentieth time, you're probably headed for the Abyss. When you're drinking all day, every day, I'd say the Abyss would be right around the corner, right after the hellified hangover. Haven't exercised in a month? Of course not! You've been too busy packing for your stay in the Abyss. Neglecting your responsibilities? Hanging out too much? Overspending? Sleeping around because you just can't be alone? Watch where you step, girl. You just might trip and fall into the Abyss.

I know. I really do. You've been through a lot. You are sooo, so tired. I know you are. And sad, so sad. You finally thought you'd found the One, didn't you? And now, now you have to start all over again. But you don't have it in you now, and you can't even begin to conceive of how you ever will. You don't feel like moving forward. No, not at all. You just want to wallow in the loss, feel sorry for yourself for a while, right? Of course you do, boo-boo. And you can, you will, and, yes, you should. Go ahead. Feel sorry for yourself. That's right. Stay home and watch sad movies. Obsess about the relationship with your girls. And please, by all means, cry your eyes out. Sleep late when you can. You deserve it. You've been through hell. Just remember not to take it *there,* to that place where the entire world is dark and depression is your blanket from the cold, cruel world. Don't do it. Don't play yourself. Life does go on, with or without a man, with or without *that* man.

Right now it's all about choices. Your choices. Everything you do is crucial to how you will recover from this
devastation. The first step is to avoid that dangerous, decep-
tive Abyss. What is the Abyss again? It is darkness. So go
ahead, dry your tears and walk toward the light.

No, I'm not preaching (yet!). I'm just telling you like it
is. When you choose to do things that will inevitably make
you feel worse, you are heading straight for the Abyss.
When you do things that will only ultimately hurt or hinder
you, via your body, mind, or spirit, in the long run you are
heading for the Abyss. So why not choose to do things that
you know are going to make you feel better? Really. Think
about it. When was the last time you went to the gym and
regretted it? Never. Every time you go, especially if you
have the time to sit in the steam room and/or sauna after a
workout, you say to yourself, "I am so glad I dragged myself
out to the gym." Don't you? Of course you do. So even if
you have to haul yourself there and go into the place evil and
mad, you will leave clearheaded. You'll still be hurt and
heartbroken, but you will surely feel better than you did before you walked through that door.

So, seriously. When was a hot bubble bath a mistake? Or
an invigorating jog around the block? Or a manicure? Or a
prayer session? Think about it. Things that are good for you
are a really good idea right about now.

You're vulnerable, if you didn't already know. This relationship's end has already left you in somewhat of a rut, and in a
dark, sad place. Why choose to do things that are going to

keep you in that place or take you deeper? Why not choose to do things that are going to help you out of that dark place and assist you in rising above the sadness so you can continue optimistically on to the next phase of your life?

There are many things you can do to avoid the Abyss, but the main thing is to use the power of positivity. To be positive you must avoid negativity at all costs, which, in our cynical society, will be far from easy. People are continually talking about and criticizing others. Or saying what they would have done or would do in such and such situations. This one is old. This one is mean. This one is stupid. Usually people who talk bad about other people all of the time are really unhappy and unsatisfied with themselves. These are the people you should steer away from seeking any advice or solace from. They can't give you anything truly positive to hold on to; they don't even know what positivity is. Also, try your best to steer your mind away from negative, dark thoughts because they only lead to negative, dark actions! This is where prayer comes in handy, as in "Good Lord, give me strength." If you are not careful, consciously guarding your thoughts, you could end up being that woman—the one physically fighting with the new girlfriend, or scratching up his car, or messing with his credit. Things that, by the way, could land you arrested or in jail. I know it can be fun to fantasize about doing mean things to hurt the guy who hurt you, but it's not worth it. Ever. One weekend I was home watching Lifetime movies and this woman actually killed her ex by knocking him off his bike with her truck! I admit it was wicked fun and made for entertaining television, but I couldn't help think to myself—*Is it really that deep?* I mean, the woman in the movie had the right to be mad (I think her husband cheated on her with her manicurist or maid or something), but where he was an adulterer, she became a murderer! Now, really. So don't even go there —to that place where you are scheming to hurt him, putting yourself in a position where you can sleep with him one last time, or reverting to self-destructive behavior. These will only sabotage your attempts at avoiding the Abyss.

The following are just a few scenarios I created to make my point and are situations you should try to avoid at all costs. Because after you do something stupid, destructive, or self-destructive, you're only going to be mad at yourself, and then where will you be? Oh, right. You'll be back in the Abyss.

Self-Sabotage Scenarios

SCENARIO #1

GIRLFRIEND #1: "Hey, girl. Are you ready?"

GIRLFRIEND #2: "Nah . . . I don't think I'm going anywhere tonight."

GIRLFRIEND #3: "What? Aw, c'mon. This is the third weekend in a row you've stayed in. I thought you said you were finally ready to get out of the house tonight.

Aren't you tired of your bed yet? I'm telling you, this party is going to be fabulous, a chance to do some real networking!!!"

GIRLFRIEND #2: "Chile, I don't care about networking. I don't have the energy to be in people's faces tonight. I'm not in the mood. I'm just going to stay home."

GIRLFRIEND #1: "Again? This is getting tired, I gotta tell ya. And I hate to think of you there all alone feeling sorry for yourself over that man."

GIRLFRIEND #2: "Well, I am feeling sorry for myself. But I am not alone!!! Shoot. I've got this movie to keep me warm, and it and me are gonna be juuuust fine tonight!!" (chuckles hysterically)

GIRLFRIEND #1: "All right. Well, enjoy your evening. I have a few new magazines I can drop by for you on my way to the party."

GIRLFRIEND #2: "No. No. That's all right. I'm going to watch this movie and go to sleep. Call me tomorrow."

She hangs up the phone and clicks on the television. She then heads into her kitchen and grabs a bag of chocolate-chip cookies and a vat of ice cream. When she returns to the television, there it is, a handsome couple locked in a sweet embrace. Tears fill her eyes as she climbs into the bed, pulls the cover over herself, and digs into her high-fat, high-calorie, too-late-at-night snack.

Staying home and feeling sorry for yourself is not the end of the world. It's a natural, maybe even necessary, response to overwhelmingly painful situations. But when it becomes a habit, when it is something that you find yourself doing over and over again, weekend after weekend, there is a problem. There is nothing wrong with wanting to be alone, with not wanting to go out and be surrounded by noisy, drunk people at a nightclub just because it's a Saturday night. But in this scenario, the woman could have chosen to be more constructive, to make herself feel better even if she was enjoying her at-home-alone time. In this case, she is going to wake up feeling guilty and lethargic, which may perpetuate the cycle and end up making her more depressed. If she is not careful, she can find herself right there, in the same spot, wallowing in her bed, eating fattening foods night after night after night. Instead, she could have used the evening to better herself by possibly pampering herself. She could have soaked her feet and given herself a pedicure while watching her movie, or done some stretches, or put on a face mask, or done her nails, or oiled, curled, or twisted her hair. She could have done something other than just feel sorry for herself. Something that would help her avoid the Abyss. She could have eaten some sorbet as opposed to ice cream, or, better yet, she could have enjoyed her movie while munching on grapes or cucumber slices or low-fat popcorn. That is what avoiding the Abyss is all about: making self-loving, self-strengthening choices despite your feelings of sadness and despair.

SCENARIO #2

It is a chilly winter night on a quiet, tree-lined residential block. At 1:30 A.M. the streets are still and silent until a black Honda pulls into a driveway where a beautiful, brand-new Jaguar sits gleaming in the night. The Honda pulls up beside it and comes to a full stop. Two slim, feline figures dressed in black occupy the Honda's front seat. Almost immediately after the car comes to a full stop, the passenger side of the car opens and out jumps one of the feline figures. The identity of this person is unclear, as the face is covered by a wool ski mask. Quickly and with agility, the figure uses the spray can in its hand to paint the word "bastard" on both sides of the Jaguar. Just as quickly, she pulls out a blade and plunges it deeply into the two front tires, the air hissing from them like a cat in heat. The figure then jumps into the awaiting Honda, which then pulls away as slowly and as quietly as it pulled up, disappearing into the dark, cold night. A few seconds later, a patrol car races up the block behind the Honda. When the sirens are heard, the Honda pulls over, and the two women in the car are arrested for vandalism.

Now why would this grown woman go and do something so trifling and pointless? Okay, maybe she was angry as hell. Maybe this guy really hurt her. But what ever happened to karma? What goes around comes around, knowing that if someone has mistreated you, he will, in one way or another, get what's coming to him, and you don't have to raise a finger.

It's just a fact of life. It's just the way it is. And what ever happened to believing in the passage "Vengeance is mine, sayeth the Lord," putting things in God's hands and knowing, trusting that He will take care of it in due time, in a way that will do much more harm than you ever could? Because what is vandalizing his car really going to do besides make her look crazy, make him glad that the relationship is over, and make him happy that he got as far away from her craziness as he could? But maybe, in her defense, it wasn't her idea. Maybe she was dumb enough to let her silly friend (and we all have one) talk her into doing something that was out of character. That's still no excuse, because she is still going to be apprehended by the police. And really, that means legal fees, time off from work, fines, maybe even jail time. Gimme a break. We do not live in the movies. Life is not a scene from *Medea* or a Terry McMillan movie. If you destroy property, you will pay for it. It's not worth it. Use that anger and aggression on something productive. Although she is obviously in the anger stage of her recovery, this woman and her girlfriend should have taken a kickboxing class that night. Or, if she was that mad, she could have thrown some dishes in her own house. Something, anything other than acting out like a child and not representing herself as a woman with class and common sense, which is something we all can and should do at all times, no matter what, under any and all circumstances.

SCENARIO #3

Int. Karen's Apartment—Early Evening

The apartment is clean and quiet except for slow jazz music playing from the stereo. The apartment is stylishly decorated and could be a page from a magazine except for the four of five large boxes sitting in the entryway.

The doorbell rings.

Karen, an attractive African-American woman in her early thirties, emerges from her bedroom wearing a beautiful nightgown that accentuates her full figure. Her long, wavy hair cascades down her back, and her full, pouty lips are highlighted by just a touch of gloss. After checking herself in the mirror, then adjusting her bosom so it will not be ignored, she opens the door.

James, a tall, dark-skinned African-American man in his early forties, is at the door.

KAREN

Hey, it's eight-thirty. You're right on time.

JAMES

(pushing past her without even a glance)
Yeah. Thanks for letting me come by to get the
rest of my stuff. I know you have other things to do.
(He picks up one of the boxes.)
I'll have these out of your way before you know it.

KAREN
Oh, okay . . .

James takes the box out to the car and returns to find Karen in the kitchen.

Int. Kitchen—Early Evening

KAREN
I made a little something, just in case you were hungry.

JAMES
No, Karen. I'm not hungry. I don't want any food.
I don't want . . . anything. I came to get
my things, and then I'm leaving.

KAREN
Oh, okay. I just thought maybe we could talk.

JAMES
I didn't think there was anything else to talk about.

KAREN
(cautiously)
We can talk about, well, about us.

JAMES
(callously)
Last I checked, there was no us.

KAREN
Don't say that.

JAMES
But it's the truth, Karen, and you know it.

KAREN
Can't we work it out?

JAMES
I . . . I really don't think so. I don't think there is anything
left to say or anything left to do.

KAREN
(seductively)
Now, c'mon, James, there has to be something we can do.
We can't just end it like this. I love you too much.

Karen slowly approaches James and drapes her arms
around his shoulders as her robe falls open to reveal her
ample bosom. She begins to nibble on his ear and kiss his
strong neck.

Int. Living Room—Evening

KAREN

I love you so much, baby. Please don't go. I love you.

James says nothing as he maneuvers the robe off her shoulders. They kiss passionately, then fall to the carpeted floor, where they make passionate, hungry love. When they are done, they lie bare in each other's arms. James is asleep, but Karen is not; she is smiling and content in his arms. Slowly, James awakens and glances halfheartedly at his watch.

JAMES

(jumping up)

Oh, man, it's nine o'clock!!! Damn!!!

KAREN

What is it, baby?

JAMES

I've got to get out of here. I need to get this stuff back to the crib, and then we have to catch our flight to Miami.

(He grabs his underpants, puts them on, and then does the same with his pants and shirt.)

KAREN

What are you talking about? Flight to Miami? And who
is we?

JAMES

Huh? Oh, nothing, nobody. Don't worry about it.

KAREN

What do you mean don't worry about it??!
You just made love to me, and now
you're taking some other woman to Miami.

JAMES

(still getting his things together)
Ah, c'mon, Karen. We both know I didn't
make love to you. . . . And I'm not taking some
other woman to Miami; I'm taking *my* woman to
Miami, all right? So let's not start any crap.
I came to get my stuff. Now I've got it, and now I'm out.

He grabs the last box by the door and leaves the apartment,
where Karen lies sobbing, naked and alone, on her living-
room floor.

If this were a scene playing in a movie, I would be the
one yelling at the screen as soon as she started to se-
duce him, as soon as they started kissing. I'd be
yelling, "Don't do it, girl, don't do it!" Because there

is no way it could have turned out well. I mean, really, her ex is coming by to pick up his stuff? And she chooses then to sleep with him? What did she think, he was going to change his mind? If she were doing it just for herself, if she just wanted to be with him one last time, it would have been understandable though ill-advised. But through her actions it was clear that was not the case. It was clear that she wanted more, that she wanted to reconcile. But instead of saying this and being honest with her feelings and having an honest conversation outside of the bedroom, she chose to sleep with him and put herself in a vulnerable position where she could be—and was—hurt and disappointed all over again. Despite her obvious feelings of loneliness and horniness, she should have protected herself emotionally. We can only hope that she protected herself physically, especially since she found out he was seeing another woman after they slept together. But whether or not she knew he was seeing another woman, she knew he hadn't been with her recently. She had no real idea what he had been doing since they split, so she should have protected herself. But with the passion and spontaneity of the scene, I, unfortunately, seriously doubt it. So now this dear woman, being impetuous and irresponsible, has put her emotional and physical well-being in jeopardy. She is clearly in the bargaining stage of her breakup, but unfortunately she is not actively avoiding the

Abyss. In fact, I have a feeling she is headed straight into it, if she isn't already there.

You have the power to create the vibe you want to have all around you by choosing your thoughts and words carefully and surrounding yourself with people whom you can talk openly and honestly with about your loss, people who themselves are positive thinkers and will help you see the brighter side of things. Now, I know it won't be easy. I know you are mad, angry, and pissed all the way off!!! You are not feeling positive; you're feeling very negative. Regardless, try not to talk negatively about your ex. That doesn't mean you can't speak the truth, as in "He hurt me" or "I am confused and disappointed" or "He is a dishonest person." But you can make a conscious effort to steer clear of saying stuff like "I hate his a—" or "I hope he gets run over by a Mack truck."

Words are powerful, and what you put out there only comes back to you. So regardless of how ugly things may have become during the relationship's downfall, when you think of and speak of him, find it in your heart to say, "God bless you," or if you prefer, "I release you," no matter how much he hurt you with his words or actions. Isn't this the person you were in love with and probably still are in love with? When you choose to say "God bless you," you are continually reminded of the divinity of this difficult situation. You are forced to focus on the fact that God has a hand in your life, and He clearly did not want this person for you. Maybe it was just a transitional relationship and wasn't supposed to last forever. Maybe it was in essence an experience you needed to prepare you for Mr. Right, your true partner. The relationship could have been a tool used by God to show you the best and worst in yourself. Saying "God bless you" is essentially an affirmation of faith, an acknowledgment that although you are hurt, disappointed, and even devastated, you accept that things happen for a reason and according to God's plan. It will be hard, but it will get easier and it will make you feel good. Really. Saying "God bless you" or "I release you," as opposed to "Screw you" or whatever else, is good for you. It stops you and your negative painful thoughts right there. Saying "Screw you" and wishing him ill will only prolong your feelings of anger and resentment. Say "Screw you," and you will find it can go on and on in your mind, as in "Screw you because you did such and such and said this and that. . . ." It's like a vicious cycle. Next thing you know, you are reliving arguments, re-experiencing stress and frustration, putting yourself through a situation that already happened some time ago over and over and over again. While your thoughts are lodged in the past and your memory spins out of control, your heart rate rises, your blood pressure goes up, you grit your teeth, your head starts to hurt, and, and . . . he's nowhere around. And you're walking around alone with a screw face for no real tangible reason. Just by saying "Screw you," you've gone and done it to yourself, made yourself sick, made yourself upset, made yourself a little older a little faster.

But saying "God bless you" is essentially letting go. It's removing yourself from the situation. It's preserving your sanity and peace of mind because it stops you from obsessing on things that happened in the past, on things you cannot change. Saying "God bless you" is better for you. And I hope you know it's all about you right now.

So try it. Right now. Say out loud, "God bless you, [ex's name]." Okay. Now say, "Screw you, [ex's name]." The latter may have been more effective in letting out your aggressions, but the first inevitably calmed you, made you feel better, more beautiful, less bitter. And that's what avoiding the Abyss is about: preventing yourself from becoming another angry, bitter woman. There are enough of those in the world already, don't you think so? I know so.

So essentially, avoiding the Abyss is all about choosing whether or not you want to be beautiful or bitter. Beware: bitterness is not only ugly and unfortunate, it's also immature. It's a refusal to accept the fact that you can't make someone love you and you can't force yourself to love someone else. It's a surrendering of sorts, an acceptance that you tried, but it just didn't work, that this one was not the One, that that phase of your life is over and you must move on to the next. Being bitter is also an assumption that no one has ever been hurt but you, and that of course is not the case. If you don't avoid the desire to pity yourself, self-destruct, become disillusioned, distrustful, and doubtful, you will wake up one day and be a bitter bitch. And then there will be no turning back. So right now, take a deep breath and make your choice. Bitterness or beauty?

You choose beauty, don't you? Of course you do. Because deep down inside, you know that life goes on and you want to fully be present, and pleasant, in what is left of it. So you choose beauty because truth cannot be denied and the truth is this: you are beautiful. And you know it. And you also know this: it's not easy being beautiful!! It's so much easier to be ugly, mean, and mad. It's so much easier to take the low road than the high road. But you've made your choice and now you have to stick with it. Now you have to fight.

The hardest battle will inevitably be with yourself and your self-esteem. Even if you really do know you are beautiful, valuable, and vibrant, you might have to find ways to remind yourself of these things after being abandoned by a man you love or leaving a man who demeaned you, told you bad things about yourself, and made you feel less than beautiful. And if you, for whatever reason, don't recognize your beauty and your value, you will have to work hard to find it, because it is there. Even if you are not beauty-pageant material (whatever that is!), you have your own special beauty and appeal, and you need to see it, embrace it, nurture it, and know it before anyone else ever can or will. After all is said and done, the most beautiful women are the women who are confident in their appeal, regardless of their complexion, size, or whatever. If you have ever seen a woman with long, beautiful hair who looked like a piece of slop and then you witnessed a beautiful bald-headed woman working it, you will know what I mean. Because nobody is perfect. Maybe you could be taller or shorter or thinner or thicker. Some things you can change and some things you can't. Change the things you can change (if you want to) and accept the things you can't change (because you have to). I know how critical we women can be of ourselves, but look at it this way: it could be better, and it could be worse. All you have to do is step out of your house on any given day and look to the left then look to the right. There will be some woman on one side who is so alluring and attractive that you will say to yourself, "Daamn!" But all you have to do is wait a few seconds and on the other side there will be some woman who is not attractive and clearly not taking care of herself, and you will say, "Dayum!" So. The bottom line is: don't look to other people to validate your beauty. It's a waste of time and precious mental and emotional energy. Instead, work with and value what you have, and who you are. Discover, nurture, accentuate, and embrace your own beauty.

Accepting yourself for who you are—warts and all—will do wonders for your self-esteem. And without self-esteem, you suffer. You let yourself be taken advantage of. You spend time with people who are beneath you. And why wouldn't you? Your self-esteem is so low that you can't see how low you have gone! So try to get that together once and for all. Do whatever you have to do to identify and deal with any deep-seated, childhood-related issues that are hindering your self-esteem. If it was a condescending mother, forgive her so you can move on. If it was a sexually abusive uncle, forgive him (no matter how hard it may be, and you may need help with this) so that you can move on and enjoy your precious wonderful life unencumbered by low self-esteem, living with and accepting only high standards for yourself and those who surround you.

After you deal with your self-esteem, you'll have to face your demons. Postbreakup is a dangerous time to have demons. You have a void in your life, and by all means you intend to find a way to fill it. At this very vulnerable place you will discover that all of your old demons come back to haunt you. Trying to stop gambling? It will be so much harder to stop at this point. Been fighting a drinking problem? The battle with the bottle will only get harder. Quit smoking last year? Yeah, but that man made you mad, and one cigarette sure would taste good right about now. Lost weight this winter? Sure you did, but you don't care. You don't care about anything anymore except devouring that pint of Chunky Monkey ice cream!!!

Right now, you want to know one thing and only one thing: what difference does it all make? Does it even matter? You lost all that weight, stopped smoking, or worked on the relationship harder, and he still left you, still you had to walk away, still the relationship didn't work. So you figure if you can't have your man, you can at least have your joint/drink/entire chocolate cake/pill/cigarette/neighbor's husband (for a night)/new wardrobe you cannot afford/old boyfriend you can't stand. And you know what? You can. You can have all of those things. Go right ahead and regress so you can start all over again, so you can sabotage all of your hard work. Yeah, that's right, indulge yourself. The doctor advised you to stay away from those pain relievers, but that man has you so stressed that all you'll need is one this time, right? Wrong. One is never enough, so why even get yourself started? Why not keep on being strong? You more than anybody else know how hard it was to get it together in the first place, and now you want to go right back to all of that? Be my guest, but first let me tell you this one thing: you're playing yourself. Don't you know that pain purifies the soul? Can't you see that this is only temporary? Haven't you realized that hurting yourself only, well, hurts yourself? I think you know the answer to all of these questions, and I know you're stronger than you think. I bet if you just tried a little to fight these urges, you could. The result? A better, smarter, stronger self. And that's a priceless thing.

So you have to prepare to fight to get better, be better, stay better. You'd better, because life does go on, and you will bump into him or someone he knows, and if you are an overweight, drugged-out adulteress, I'll find you and slap you myself!!! Because I may not know who you are, but I know that if you picked up this book, you are special and smart. I know that if you are reading this book, you want to deal with this situation in a different way, a better way, a healthier way, a more positive way. You want to be the best woman you can be no matter who walks out of your life, regardless of whom you choose to walk away from. So when you made the choice to stay beautiful, you made the choice to be strong and to utilize that strength to make the right choices. Think about it. When you lost those ten pounds last year, you had to be strong enough not to eat late, right? When you got that degree two months ago, you were strong enough to stay home and study, despite the kids and the dinner and the dishes, weren't you? So you know that anything worth having is hard work, is worth fighting for. And right now you're fighting for you—the whole, healthy, and uniquely beautiful you.

So no matter how depressed, angry, pissed, mad, lonely, hurt, evil, lost, alone, and confused you feel, get up and take that spin class you've been taking for the past six months. That's right. Keep on doing what you've been doing as long as it's a good thing. Avoiding the Abyss means doing good things you do not feel like doing but doing them anyway. Sewing class on Thursdays? You'll be there! Why wouldn't you be? Were you and your ex taking ballroom dancing once a week? Go, even if it means you have to dance with the instructor. Started taking French lessons in preparation for your romantic honeymoon in Paris? Well, there may not be any honeymoon with him, but there might be with someone else, or you might take the trip alone or with friends, so you will have your pretty self right in that class on Saturday, won't you? Of course you will. Sticking to your routine is mandatory now. Your relationship is over, but that does not give you an excuse to just stop. Trust me, the last thing you want to do is to give yourself extra time to wallow in self-pity and depression. You have enough time to do that, and you do it every chance you can. That's right. There's no shame in your game, and there doesn't need to be. Heartbreak is painful and real. You don't feel like going to class, work, or church. You just want to stay in your bed, and you can. For now. But you can't do it forever. I know it seems like your heart will never heal, but it will. It might even get stronger in the process. I know you can't see past your disappointment right now to even glimpse that reality, but it is so true. You know how I know? Because I've been there, too. My heart has been broken on more than a few occasions, thank you. Some of them have simply been disappointments, no big deal, but still, me being human, I was hurt.

Just recently I was dating a guy whom I was really feeling. We had been dating for a few months and things were going relatively well until he told me he wanted to date other people. I was mad. I was annoyed. I didn't love him, we weren't even intimate, it was only a Level One relationship, and I definitely wasn't devastated, but I still ended up asking myself questions like "What's wrong with me?" "Will I ever find the right man?" etc., etc. So on the Saturday after he broke it off with me, I found myself moping around the house feeling sorry for myself. I didn't want to talk to any of my friends, didn't want to be bothered with anyone at all. I just wanted to sleep. And that's exactly what I did; I slept all day. But the next day I wasn't feeling much better. It was a sunny Sunday, but I had no desire to get up, get dressed, and go to church. I envisioned myself lying in the bed, watching television, and eating; basically wasting another God-given gift of a beautiful day. I knew I couldn't do it. I had to do something that would deflect the oncoming depression. I had to avoid the Abyss! So I got up, showered, put on my prettiest dress, and went to church. I didn't realize until I had gotten there that it was Easter Sunday! In my funk, I had forgotten, and since my daughter had been spending a few days with her father, I had been in my own little world. But needless to say, after church I was feeling like the fabulous, blessed, beautiful woman who I am, so I fluttered over to my grandmother's home, where my lovingly neurotic family greeted me. Their smiles, jokes, and Grandma's good food all made me feel great, and when I finally left, I felt a million times better. By simply forcing myself to do something positive—go to church—I avoided the Abyss, went ahead with my life, and haven't looked back since (well, except now, to tell you about it).

But there was a specific liaison—I won't call it a relationship—that really devastated me, that really blew my friggin' mind to the point where I could not see how I would get over it. Avoid the Abyss? Ladies, I *was* the Abyss. Sold tickets to my sad show. Reveled in my misery and depression. Drank. Slept. Cried. Whined. Overate. Underachieved. Stayed on the phone obsessing over him for hours with anyone who would listen. Called him and hung up a million times (who cares about caller ID? Not me!). Wrote him letters and tore them up. I think I even broke a few glasses. 'Cause I was mad at him and mad at myself for being caught up in such a trifling relationship with such a disgusting man.

This is what happened. I was hanging out with some

girlfriends one evening at a small local club where a friend of ours would occasionally DJ. When he did his sets, we would usually try to go show him our support. It was supposed to be a pretty early night because it was a weekday and we all had to get up in the morning. So there we were, enjoying the music and catching up with one another, when I saw this fine, tall Djimon Hounsou–looking creature looking at me! Well. I smiled and batted my eyes and he came over and we ended up hanging out for the rest of the night. No. I didn't take him home and I didn't sleep with him. Well, actually I did, but it was a few weeks later. Still, it was too soon because I didn't give myself a chance to really get to know him, to really recognize his character traits, to really see what I was getting myself into.

Well, anyway, I was on my way into the rabbit hole and after dating for two months he said he wanted us to be exclusive, to "go together," to be a couple. Which—as every woman should know—is a red flag. If a man moves too fast he usually has commitment issues or his own self-esteem issues. I don't know which one, but I know he has issues and you should be wary. I didn't know this at the time. I sure did learn it the hard way. I was surprised by his proposition because so far what we had was fun and casual and I was enjoying things the way they were. I told him this, but he was insistent that he was in loooove and we should be together. So we started going out. He was a good boyfriend too. Liked to take me out and show me off. Liked to talk late into the night. Liked a lot of the music and movies I liked. He helped me move furniture, hang pictures, carry groceries. I became comfortable and was happy to have him around as this was the first real "relationship" I had been in after ending things with my daughter's father. He gave me money, picked me up from work, and took me out to nice dinners. All the while he was actively sleeping with and pursuing other women. I didn't know it at the time until he started to show the signs. You know, saying he's coming over at a certain time and not showing up until hours later with a lame excuse. Or worse, not showing up at all. I went into the ever-available Queen of Denial mode and found ways to believe his lies and make excuses for his behavior in my mind, especially when, if I voiced my concerns and suspicions about his behavior, he would say, "Put some trust in me, Kerika." And so I did. After all, he'd said he was in loooove with me.

One Friday night, though, when he called to tell me he was not coming over and was going to stay in because he was tired from working all day then coming home and doing all his laundry, I went into a trance. I knew his voice didn't sound quite right. I knew he wasn't telling me the truth. Next thing I knew I was at his house, and believe me, it really was a trance, because I, in my right mind, would never go to a man's house unannounced. But against my better judgment, I went anyway. And when I got to his apartment building, the door was wide open. I see it now as divine intervention. His downstairs neighbors were having a party, and people were coming in and going out. So where I would usually have to ring his bell to get in, this time I just went in. When I walked up the stairs to his apartment, I already knew. I approached his door slowly, leaned my ear on the door, and heard a female voice talking. I knocked on the door. After a few seconds, he opened the door nonchalantly. He clearly was expecting someone who lived in the building, because no one was buzzed in. But it wasn't a neighbor. It was me. When he saw me, he was shocked, tried to smile, then pulled his robe closed. (Yes, yes, y'all, he was wearing a robe with nothing on underneath!) I jumped up, mushed him in the face, told him he was full of you know what, then fled down the steps before he could mush me back or worse. By the time I'd reached the bus stop, he was hot on my heels in a thrown-on sweat suit and sneakers. He said something about being sorry, she was just a friend, and maybe I should come upstairs and meet her. I wasn't going for it. As much as I wanted to, I knew I couldn't, shouldn't believe him. I was so damn mad, but I wasn't even mad at him as much as I was mad at myself. I had never been in a situation like that. That was something off of a Jerry Springer show or something. I mean, I went to Howard University, for goodness' sake, and never experienced any trifling "My man was in the room with another woman and I went over there and . . ." crap. Ugh. I was incensed. It was so not my scene.

This experience is really why, to this day, I try my best not to judge people or talk about them, because you never know when it can be you in the same situation. In the past I have had friends who had caught their man doing whatever with whomever and although I was supportive, a part of me couldn't help but think, *Well, damn, how blind do you have to be?* But that was because I had never been in that situation myself. I couldn't sympathize with being seduced and lied to by a man who claimed to love you only to have him turn around and cheat on you. I've had boyfriends who have come out and told me they wanted to see other people, and man, after what I went through with this man, did I respect them for it. My feelings may have been hurt, but at least I knew I was dealing with someone with some kind of integrity. Because the liars and cheaters—oh! My skin was crawling. I was disgusted with him, and I was disgusted with myself.

Still, after that incident I found myself thinking about him, even missing him. I started to wonder what I lacked that made him go to another woman. I started to doubt myself, my appeal, my beauty. My mind was playing tricks on me. It was crazy. He was always on my mind and often in my dreams, even after it was over, even after I stopped seeing him. I would joke with my friends and say stuff like, "Y'all, I think he put an African hubba-jubba on me!" but a part of me wasn't joking. A part of me was really serious, because what the . . . ! The reality was that it was hard for me to move on from the situation because it honed in on some of my most personal issues of self-doubt and diffidence. To this day, I find that this is the relationship that has been the most transforming for me because I was so hurt, confused, and shocked I had to ask myself some real hard questions about myself, about what I was willing to accept in a relationship and what I was not. I had to wonder why I chose to look the other way when I knew he wasn't being sincere. Why did I not trust my instincts? Why did I allow myself to be taken advantage of in this way? Was a relation-ship—a man—so important that I would let myself be used and lied to? It was a turning point for me in a way because for the first time I had to address my issues of insecurity and reassess my self-worth.

Eventually, inevitably, I had to get a grip. On myself, my emotions. My life. I realized that while time does heal wounds, I had to take an active role in my recovery.

Once when I was home feeling sorry for myself over the sorry state of my relationship, an Afro-Caribbean class at the local gym literally saved my life. I was really depressed, had been in the house all day. I was numb. Comatose. Damn near suicidal. Yes. There goes that word. We're not supposed to think about it, let alone talk about it, but it's real. It's pathetic, it's stupid, it's sad, but it's real. In those dark moments when you ask yourself what's the point, why bother, why keep trying, or those moments where faith is not enough, recognize that any thoughts of suicide are not right and extremely dangerous. I know I did. I mean I knew I wasn't going to "go there" and off myself over some phi-landering fool, but the simple fact that the thought even crossed my mind scared me to my senses. I jumped up. Pulled off my funky robe, threw on some clean sweats and sneakers, and ran, and I mean ran, to the gym. I didn't look at the schedule so I had no idea what kind of class was going on, but thankfully, when I got there, an Afro-Caribbean dance class was just beginning. God is good. The class was funky and fun and invigorating and just what I needed. What made the class truly a blessing was the spirit and temperament of the instructor. She was a mature woman of about fifty, with an amazing body and long dreadlocks, whose energy was infectious. Her demeanor was very necessary for me at that particular time because if it had been a corny, uninspiring instructor I probably would have just gone through the motions and remained trapped in my head with my crazy thoughts. But she wasn't having any of that. I was stiff and sad and lazy and she saw it.

"Let it go!" she demanded over the sound of the live drummers who were playing. "Throw your head back!" she shouted. "Give it up!" was her command. It was amazing. Talk about shaking it off!!

I was so glad I went to the gym that evening, and to this day I consider that woman an angel, a blessing from above. Before that class I was feeling sorry for myself. Afterward, I was laughing at myself. Before that class I was so confused. Afterward? Clearheaded. Before that class I was feeling fat. Afterward? Fabulous! I walked out of that class as a living, breathing, smiling (and sweating) example that exercise is the ultimate mood enhancer. This is due to the effects of endorphins—powerful hormone-like substances produced in the brain that function as the body's own natural painkillers. When we exercise—walk, dance, run, jump, play ball, work the elliptical machine, whatever—our body produces endorphins and we end up feeling much better than we did prior to our physical activities. I know I did! After that experience I made it a point to do some type of physical activity as often as I could. Don't get me wrong; I didn't turn into an "exercise addict"—a person who actually loves the effects that exercise has on his or her mood and outlook so much that all he or she ever wants to do is exercise. No. That's not me. I'm not obsessed. I'm just convinced that exercising is essential to my own happiness and well-being and am committed to finding healthy ways to make myself feel better when I get down, so that I will never get down as low as I was that day.

This experience reminded me of what I already knew: that the time after a relationship's end could and should be a time for healing, renewal, and even rebirth. Relationships, even the best ones, take a lot out of you. This one took a whole lot out of me. I had to get it back, to get myself back. And I did. I came up with a recovery plan and stuck to it. It wasn't easy, but it was worth it. Because, baby, after being depressed, despondent, down in the dumps, and losing myself to the situation, there's nothing like the light; there's nothing like finding yourself and remembering who you really are. There's nothing like being back!

If, unlike it was for me, a dance class is not enough motivation, and you find that you really can't get it together, can't get off the couch, can't clean your house, can't seem to put anything beneficial to your body into your mouth, just can't, there is one more thing you can do: leave. Pack a bag for a long weekend and go stay with a good friend or understanding family member. Hopefully it will be just for a few days, but you may need more time. You may really need someone to help you, to get you tea, to pray with you, to take you for a walk or at least open a window in the room you'll be sleeping in all day. And even if the person you stay with is unable to coddle you (people do have their own lives, you know), you will be forced to do little things that will help you at this time. Seriously. It's real hard not to shower or at least wash your face or brush your teeth if you're staying at someone else's place. You see, because when you are at home, you're at home. Your home. Where no one can tell you what to do 'cause you are grown and you pay the bills and if you wanna be mad and sad and funky on your own couch in your own house that's exactly what you are going to do.

You could easily have someone come stay with you, but that's defeating the purpose. You need to get out of your physical space so you can get out of your mental space. Sometimes your home, no matter how beautiful and well-decorated, can be too familiar, especially if you lived with or spent a lot of time there with your ex. Another suggestion is to treat yourself to a three-day vacation if you can afford it. It doesn't have to be anywhere special. It can be somewhere in your very own city or town. Maybe go to an inn or even rent a nice hotel room for a long weekend. Take some books and magazines. Whatever. Just don't forget your journal. Get a massage. Or don't. The point is, if you can do it, do it—Get Out Of YOUR House! No matter how comfortable it is. Even if it's just for one night. You have to jump-

start your recovery process. You need different scenery. So
even if circumstances do not allow you to get up, get out, get
away, go into another room. Used to sleeping in the bedroom? Camp out on the couch! Do whatever you can do
with your resources to make your space feel different. Move
a mirror. Reposition your bed. You need to give this whole
thing a new perspective, to really make the conscious decision to commit to your recovery like you were committed to
your relationship.

NEWSFLASH: Avoiding the Abyss is easier said
than done! You can be reading this and say to yourself, "Avoid the Abyss?!! Too late. I'm in the Abyss. That's
right, I've fallen and I can't get up." If you've got it bad and
have not managed to avoid the Abyss and find that you are
really stuck, you have to take action. You have to get a push,
the push you have not been able to give yourself. Maybe
you should see a therapist or talk with your pastor. Most
churches have free or low-cost counseling that you can take
advantage of. Some cities have toll-free numbers where you
can speak to someone about your grief. This is especially
true if you have experienced thoughts of suicide on a regular
basis. In this case you might need real help, like visits with a
psychotherapist who can prescribe mood stabilizers or anti-
depressants. You may have a chemical imbalance. And between menopause and menstruation and PMS, it could be
hormones. If you are adverse to prescription drugs, try visiting a holistic-health practitioner who can offer alternatives
to drugs. But don't take any chances if these thoughts per-

sist. Because no matter how hurt and heartbroken you are, suicidal thoughts are not healthy or normal. These thoughts are extremely dangerous and a sign that your grief may go deeper than you think. These thoughts are unacceptable and should be addressed professionally through whichever method you think is best, be it traditional or alternative medicine, immediately.

Chapter 4

YOU ARE NOT ALONE

*"The Lord is nigh unto them that are of a broken
heart; and saveth such as be of contrite spirit."*
Psalm 34:18

As you prepare to move through the stages of recovering from your relationship, please remember one thing: the most important relationship you can ever have is the one you have with God. If you can remember that, it will put things in perspective for you. Regardless of your religion, you will find this is a comforting reality. While living through this painful experience and having feelings of despair, loneliness, and grief, remembering the fact that you are God's child and He has a plan for you and your life can only bring you the peace you so desperately crave. When you remember this, you'll also remember that you have everything you need already. It's okay to want a mate; it's your divine right to be able to share love and commitment with another human being while on this earth. I believe that we ARE supposed to be with someone. We SHOULD seek to share our lives with someone who is just as beautiful and special as we are. But any time you choose to love someone, you are stepping out on faith. The only problem is, we are human. And the person you choose to love is human. So by nature that person is unpredictable and consequently unreliable. Even if the person claims to love you or really does love you, it's human love that is affected by desires, temptations, ideas, personal demons, fears, past pain and/or loss, childhood abuse, and countless other issues.

Human love is mercurial; it is always changing. Sometimes for better but sometimes for worse. Therefore, the only love you can really count on is the love of God. It is always there. It has no conditions. It just is. It's not moody, restless, or unfaithful. It's unwavering. It's exactly what you need, when you need it. The comfort and peace only the Most High can provide is right in your heart. It's always with you. Although, yes, I know there is nothing like the strong arms of a man holding you. And yes, of course we have physical needs that are real, for real! But we also have spiritual needs that are real. Pay attention to those right now. Feed your spirit. When you find yourself in a situation that is painful, you know the only way out is through a strong spirit. Trusting in God, being obedient, being clear enough to hear what your next move should be are mandatory so that you do not get any more lost than you already are. So be still. Say a prayer. Listen to your inner voice. I believe that voice is the voice of God in you. God guiding you. God loving you. And when you listen to that voice you can't go wrong.

Sometimes I can't help but think that God gives us heartache and disappointment in our lives in order to bring us closer to Him. To humble us. To make us stop and be still, if only for a sweet second. We're always running and reaching. A broken heart can stop you in your tracks and force you to reassess yourself and your choices, while ultimately refortifying your relationship with the Creator. In this way, your breakup can be viewed as a blessing in disguise. Having a close relationship with God makes the good times great and the bad times bearable. Because at the end of the day, it is God who hears your inner thoughts, your dreams, desires, and prayers. It is God who gives you the breath and the energy to live your life, every day. All the time. Know that God is pulling you closer to Him for a reason. Maybe He wants you to do some work on yourself. Maybe He has some work to do on you. So let Him do His thing. Let God be your strength. Let His words of wisdom and promise of salvation be the things that keep you warm at night and be the things that make you want to get out of bed in the morning. Find your favorite Bible passages. If you don't know any, ask your grandma or your next-door neighbor or your pastor or your coworker. Someone somewhere in your vicinity knows the Bible and can offer you strengthening scriptures. Or better yet, just get your hands on a Bible, say a silent prayer for guidance, and open the book. Odds are in your favor that you will turn to a scripture that addresses what you are going through at that exact moment.

For those of you who know the word, are familiar with scripture, and have a few favorites, pull them out. Say them out loud. Copy them again. Type them out on pretty paper and put them in a frame. Do anything you have to do to keep them close to you. Turn to Psalm 121: "I will lift up mine eyes unto the hills from whence cometh my help. My help cometh from the Lord, who made heaven and earth." That's it. That's the reality. You need to lean on God at this time, but most importantly at all times. "My soul finds rest in God alone; my salvation comes from him. He alone is my rock and my salvation. He is my fortress. I will never be shaken" (Psalm 62:1–2). Because, for me, believing in God is all about having faith. Faith is a powerful tool that should always be with you, especially in times of loss and confusion. Without faith, how can you go on? Without faith, why would you believe the work you have to do on yourself will be worth it?

Keeping in mind that there are many different spiritual practices and a plethora of religious beliefs, know it is not my intention to persuade you to be what I am and believe what I believe but rather to find and embrace your religion, your spiritual practices, your rituals. I was born and raised Baptist and have found my strength and support in the Baptist church ever since I was a little girl going to church with my grandmother Evelyn. But I am aware that many people have problems with the Black church, have no affinity for organized religion. As women, especially as women whose ancestral history includes servitude, slavery, and oppression, it is natural for some to feel the need to question the Bible and even understandable if you find yourself uncomfortable with some of the images and symbolism offered by the Christian church. And of course, if you don't feel like being bothered with all the people politics that take place in some of the best Black churches, who can blame you? Just don't use any of this as an excuse not to solidify and fortify your relationship with a higher power. Whether you call it Allah or Yemin-Ya or the Universe, being grounded in some sort of spirituality is going to be necessary for your recovery.

Think about Tina Turner. As depicted in the movie *What's Love Got to Do with It*, the singer was introduced to Buddhism when she was ready to leave her horribly abusive relationship with Ike Turner. But more important than her being introduced to Buddhism was that she was receptive to it. She needed something spiritual, something grounding, something that took her outside of herself so she could be quiet, so she could be still, so she could find the strength to move on. Without having something to hold on to other than herself, without her belief in something other than herself, she may not have had the strength to do what she needed to do, what was long overdue. And when she finally did what she had to do? When she finally was able to walk away? Well, we all know that she went on to be super-successful, more successful than she ever was with or even could have been with Ike. We all know that the rest was history.

Tina is one of many women that I call my *He's Gone . . . You're Back* Heroes—a woman who happily and successfully recovered from the wrong relationship, a woman who is better off now than she was then, a woman who refuses to be broken, defined, or burdened by a bad relationship. Many of my *He's Gone . . . You're Back* Heroes are well-known women I admire because of the way they handled their breakups, which were, unlike ours, played out in the public eye. Some may say that I shouldn't count them, that their situations are not the same because they are famous and have unlimited resources. Maybe that is true, and maybe—definitely—no one knows the real behind-the-scenes deal of how they handled their situation. But a human is a human and pain is pain. Money *can* buy you a month's retreat in St. Bart's, but it *can't* buy you common sense, inner strength, and an indomitable spirit.

HERE ARE SOME OF MY *HE'S GONE . . . YOU'RE BACK* HEROES:

Vanessa Williams—I guess if she could recover from being stripped of her Miss America crown after posing for nude photos and coming back to be a recording artist and an actress of stage and screen, we should have known she wasn't going to let her second ex-husband Rick Fox's public philandering stop her from shining.

Valerie Bertinelli—She let go of an abusive, drug-fueled twenty-year rocky marriage to a rock 'n' roller and went on to lose forty pounds, write and publish her memoirs, admit that she wasn't America's sweetheart after all, and show off her new man on *Oprah.* That's how you do it!

Halle Berry—She said she wanted to kill herself after her divorce from that arrogant David Justice. And she had to want to die after marrying that no-shoe-wearing, no-self-control-having Eric Benet. But I know she's glad she's living now! New boyfriend! New baby! New Halle! If anybody deserves it, she does. I'm rooting for the girl!

Nicole Kidman—Is it just me or does it seem like as soon as Tom Cruise and Nicole Kidman broke up, *her* career took off? That she was in every good movie that came out, just acting her behind off and winning Oscars? Could she possibly have been pulling herself back, allowing her superstar husband to shine while they were married, but once they broke up, she said—Bunk that! We'll never know, but that's what it seems like to me. She never spoke badly about the relationship or him in the press—except for that little *"At least now I can wear heels on the red carpet"* comment, but I'm not mad at her, are you?—and stood singly by as she and we watched him meet and marry a much younger woman and jump all up and down on Oprah's couch ranting about it. Despite her ice-princess persona, that could not have been fun to watch or easy to endure. But who's jumping up and down now? Miss Nicole, with her fellow Australian of a husband, baby girl, and Lord knows how many more films and Oscars in her future.

Iyanla Vanzant—In her many books, this Brooklyn native discusses in detail the struggles and challenges she faced being a young mother married to an abusive man. She talks about her issues growing up, her messed-up family, her personal pain and struggles. Still, she found a way to get herself and her children away from unhealthy relationships, went back to school—law school no less!!—tapped into her spirituality and writing ability, and became a bestselling author, life coach, and motivational speaker. I'm loving it!

Mary-Louise Parker—In 2003, her boyfriend, actor Billy Crudup, walked out on her after they had been dating for seven years. Okay. Ouch. That had to hurt. But there's more. He left her for a younger woman, actress Claire Danes (they are no longer together either). Hold on. That's not it. Mary-Louise Parker was EIGHT MONTHS PREGNANT with his child!!!!

I always felt so bad for her when I read about it (which had to make it worse for her, having her business all up in every newspaper). Obviously she had her baby, a son, and went on with her life and career. (By the way, what's up with Billy Crudup's career these days? Just wondering.) But I know it could not have been easy for her. Which is why I was so happy when I heard about her new boo and pending nuptials to the cutie who played Denny Duquette on *Grey's Anatomy*. If anybody deserves it, it's her. She's the poster girl for all women who have ever been hurt by a jerk! She went through the fire and made it to the other side! And even though I've heard that the relationship has ended, that there will be no wedding for these two after all, Mary-Louise Parker, you're my hero!

* * *

So you see, even celebrities—the rich, the famous, the beautiful—are not immune to heartache. Find your own *He's Gone . . . You're Back* Heroes—the famous, the infamous, and the anonymous—and use their situations as forms of inspiration, as a way to help you live out your own successful relationship-recovery story.

If you take a moment to think about it, I'm sure you know a few women in your world who went through a horrible breakup and actually survived despite seemingly insurmountable odds. I know I know a few. A good friend of mine—we'll call her Jamie—was happily married for over a decade. She was cute. He was cute. They had cute kids. They lived the cute New York lifestyle—large apartment in Harlem, attending all the art exhibits, jazz concerts, and museum galas. I adored them, was proud of them, never, ever imagined that they would not be together. Then one day after a brief trial separation I got the call from Jaime: her husband had started seeing someone else. To make matters worse, she found out by coming home only to discover the woman in her shower. Needless to say, my good friend was good and hurt. Devastated, actually. She still tried to maintain, took care of her two beautiful children, went to work. But that was it. This vibrant, fiery, sexy woman was a shell of her old self. She would call me late at night and tell me how hurt she was. She couldn't understand how it had happened, how he could hurt her the way he did. She cried a lot. It was bad. The worst part was that she still wanted him and tried unsuccessfully to reunite with him. But he was content with his new, young, foreign female friend and thought it best they keep things the way they were. What could she do? She had to accept it. It was hard, but after much heartache, pain, and prayer, she got it and got on with her life. She enrolled in school so she could make a long-overdue career change, started paying attention to her health, and started taking Bikram yoga classes diligently. To this day, she swears the sweating and breathing and stretching saved her life—gave her something to do with all her pent-up energy. She was always a petite woman, but now she was tiny, shapely, and firm. She was happy, and I was happy for her.

Then real tragedy struck. Her beloved father, whom she was very close to, died suddenly. Before she knew it, she was on a plane to Bermuda for his funeral and burial. While in Bermuda—where she grew up—she says that although it was very painful, it was peaceful. She took advantage of the nature and scenery and sunsets and seasides to say good-bye to her husband and to her father, to release all that she had lost. She says that after only a few days there—in which she did a lot of crying, praying, and even yelling at the stars—she felt her burdens lifted. Feeling a little adventurous, she accepted an invitation from some old school friends to attend the local Bermuda Jazz Festival that was wrapping up that weekend. She had been oblivious to the fact that one was going on, for obvious reasons. But she threw on a sundress, slipped into her flip-flops, pulled back her hair, and prepped herself for a night of music, comedy, drinking, and dancing. She expected to have a good time, and she did. What she didn't expect was to meet her future husband. But she did. He says when he first saw her, she had a light around her and a lightness about her. When they finally danced then talked and she told him she was divorced, he said he was surprised because in his experience most divorced women, especially recently divorced ones, usually wear a fake smile but there is sadness behind their eyes, or they try to come off fun and fearless but reveal themselves to be angry and bitter. But not my girl Jamie. She was truly, genuinely happy with herself, at peace with her painful past, ready for the future, and bam! When she was not even looking she found her future husband. I can't wait for their wedding—they're planning to hold it during the annual Bermuda Jazz Festival. I wonder why.

Another one of my *He's Gone . . . You're Back* Heroes is a wonderful colleague named Dr. Deb, well-known and respected in the field of historical and fine-art photography. Meeting and knowing Deb has been a great influence on my life. Having her look at, let alone appreciate and applaud, my work as a photographer has been one of the highlights of my life. It was Dr. Deb who gave me the opportunity to have my photos published in a book called *Black: A Celebration of a Culture,* and it was through my association with this woman that I was able to meet and have my work exhibited by the late, great Gordon Parks. I love and respect this woman because she raised a wonderful son on her own and built a successful career around photography by taking pictures, teaching, and preserving precious historical photos.

She liked to connect people and was always online e-mailing friends and associates about an upcoming exhibit or an encroaching submission deadline. She liked to share her work and the work of other photographers, and she was and remains one of the driving forces of networking and information in the Black photographers' art scene in New York.

So when she stopped answering e-mails and returning phone calls, people got a bit concerned. Where's Deb? friends wanted to know. What's up with Deb? fellow photographers inquired. I figured she was busy or traveling as usual and didn't think anything of it. Until about a month later when she sent everyone on her e-mail list a message. It was a letter apologizing for being unavailable to return phone calls and answer e-mails and explaining that her husband had left her unexpectedly. She admitted that the breakup had blindsided her and that she had taken some time to pull herself together. I was in shock. Not because of her relationship situation, but because of the honest and straightforward way she chose to deal with it. She could have just apologized for not being in touch, said something like "I have had some personal issues" and kept it at that. She didn't owe any of us any explanations, especially when it was dealing with her personal relationships. But I think this is a testament to her spirit and strength. It was the truth, and she put it out there. There was no need to sugarcoat it, hide it, or lie about it. I think her honesty was instrumental to her healing.

I saw her a few months later at an exhibit she had curated, and although she was still shaken, she looked great. She was smiling and laughing. She was also getting support and advice on the spot from all her friends and associates. Nobody felt bad about talking about it or bringing it up because she had already addressed it. It was already out there. So when I finally got a chance to catch up with her, I didn't hesitate to ask her how she was doing, how she was holding up. She admitted that she was still struggling but that she knew she was going to be all right after her son, Hank, told her, "Mom, if you could survive cancer, you can surely survive this." So there you have it. Dr. Deb. Respected historian and photographer. Mother. Cancer survivor. My *He's Gone . . . You're Back* Hero!

Who are some of your *He's Gone . . . You're Back* Heroes? It could be anybody—your best friend, your co-worker, even your eccentric auntie! Look around and see whose experiences, challenges, and triumphs you can learn and garner inspiration from. I believe God puts people in my path to act as examples, as a way of showing me that if someone else can do it—whether it be to put together an exhibit or survive a heartbreak or both—so can I. And so can you. Knowing that you are not alone helps you to eliminate anger and resentment, helps you bypass the whole "why me?" syndrome: Why did this happen to me? How could I let this happen to me? etc. Taking into consideration that this is not just happening to you and realizing that it usually at some point in life happens to everyone, men and women, Black and white, you will find that it's not so easy to fall into feeling sorry for yourself or getting sucked into self-pity. Knowing that you are not alone, that other women have survived what you are going through or worse, should be a source of strength and inspiration. That's why identifying some of your own *He's Gone . . . You're Back* Heroes is so important, so powerful.

You are not alone. Everybody has a sad story, has had a broken heart. I can't speak for many of the celebrities mentioned, but of all the everyday women I've spoken with about their relationships and recovery, each said she couldn't have done it without the belief in resurrection, rebirth, and renewal. So find or rediscover a spiritual practice that speaks to you. Embrace it. Practice it. Hold on to it as if your life depends on it, because, in many ways, it does.

NEWSFLASH: If you have a friend who is going through a breakup, it is your responsibility to let her know she is not alone. I know, she really may want to be alone and may not want to be bothered with you or anyone else. She may be taking time for herself to reflect, to relax, to recover. So what? She may be putting on a brave face, telling you she is fine. But you know she's fronting! You can still call and leave a funny and/or inspirational message on her machine. If you find a good, positive poem that you know she can relate to right now, that you know will bring a smile to her face, that you know will make her feel better, e-mail it to her or even grab an envelope, slap a stamp on it, and drop a copy in the mail! Send her flowers. Book a massage for her. Make a nice healthy salad and/or a hearty, savory soup and drop it off. Buy her an aromatic candle. Pick up her favorite bath oil. Or how about taking her kids for a night? It won't kill you. Really, it won't. Don't be overbearing or intrusive; just be there. Be available. Be her sounding board when she wants to talk and her shoulder when she wants to cry. After all, she's your friend. She's been there for you, and now you have to be there for her.

Chapter 5
YOUR TRUTH SHALL SET YOU FREE

"Truth indeed rather alleviates than hurts, and will
always bear up against falsehood, as oil does above
water."   Miguel de Cervantes

O kay, ladies. You knew the time would come eventually: The time to come clean about what *really* went
down in your relationship. The time to face your role in the
relationship's demise. The time to pinpoint the beliefs you
hold and the fears you carry and the hurts you nurse that
stood in the way of a successful relationship. The time to acknowledge your mistakes, oversights, and unnecessary
compromises. The time to admit to the ugly and the unfor-
givable. Yes, ladies. It is time to tell the truth. But don't
panic. No one has to know your truth but you. After all, it's
yours, this truth, and through your actions, thoughts,
words, and deeds, you earned it. Of course it can help to talk
about these things with friends, close family members, or
even a therapist if necessary. You might have done that already, though, telling your version of the truth, making
yourself out to be the victim (which you probably were in
some instances), avoiding the ugly details. I mean, everybody doesn't have to know everything about you and your

relationship, do they? Of course not. Only if you want them to. Other people knowing the truth about your relationship is irrelevant. You knowing the truth about your relationship is invaluable. So, my dear broken hearts, I have provided you with this space, this haven, this respite, if you will. Here you will be propelled to answer questions that, up until this instant, you might not have wanted to answer or you might not even have thought to ask. The best part is, you don't have to share these truths with anyone—not your momma, your ex-man, your new man, your friend, your coworker— if you do not want to. I really think that is one of the big blessings that comes with being born a woman. No matter how much we talk or how much we share gossip, beauty tips, or weight-loss advice—no one ever really knows our whole story except us. Like my Grandma Marie always says, *You have to have something to share on your deathbed!*

Seriously, though. In the silent corners of your mind, late at night, after you've written in your journal, or talked on the phone with your friends, or read your novel, or cried your eyes out, and there is nothing but silence—what do you hear? Silence? But there is something else. That something else, my friends, is the truth. Yes, because silence speaks, and if you listen closely, it will tell you everything you are dying to hear. But be aware that the truth is not always so easy to hear. It's drowned out by your ego and your pride and your fear of facing it. Some may speculate that it sounds different to everybody, but I disagree. It sounds like one thing and only one thing: the Damn Truth.

So come on. I know you can do it. You can answer these questions I will present to you and, more importantly, answer the questions that will be presented to you by participating in this process. I know it won't be easy, but I won't tell if you won't. You can keep the revelations to yourself or share them now, later, or on your deathbed. It's up to you. Thankfully, once you know your truth, you have already let it go—there's no real reason to share it with anyone. Once you know your truth you will recognize it when it comes up again, in a different situation (and we all know that it will). Once you know your truth, you can deal with it, accept it, laugh at it even. Yes, because when it is all revealed to you, your truth shall set you free.

Still not convinced? Still not ready to spill it, even to yourself? Need a push? Someone to start? Okay. I'll be your guinea pig. I'll start. Despite the fact that I feel I have, so far, sufficiently shared enough of my personal business with you, I will start. I will share some of my truths with you just so that you know exactly what I mean. Here goes.

I love my family, that's the truth. We are strong. We are beautiful. We are composed primarily of women. We have old Southern roots, and it has occurred to me that although we have made progress in the arts and psychology and education, we have dragged some old, antiquated ideas about men, their power, and their place in our lives right into this century. These ideas have been ingrained in me and have led me to believe, on a subconscious level, despite my cries of girl power and support of women's liberation, that men are

more important than women, that a man's life has more
value than a woman's, that a man's happiness is more important than a woman's happiness, that men have more
power than women, and that my life will always basically
suck and be lacking on some level if there is not some man
somewhere in the vicinity, regardless of how emotionally,
physically, or financially weak that man is. I know. Sad. But
true (which, remember, is the operative word here). And
how has this truth set me free, your inquiring minds want to
know? Well, now that I am aware, I can catch myself when I
find I am having unrealistic and unproductive thoughts
about relationships. For instance, if I meet a nice man and
immediately find myself fantasizing about the two of us
building a life together, I immediately remind myself that I
know absolutely nothing about him. I then make a mental
note of my life, the life I've built for myself by myself, remember that I am proud of it and value it, and realize that I
am in fact not in any real rush to compromise or even possibly jeopardize my life for some strange man. Then, the best
part is, I can laugh at myself and keep it moving.

In a moment of truth, I realized my issues with men
stemmed from so many things I was brought up with. Some
can be defined as old wives' tales. Some can be considered
myths. But in my family these things were—I mean are!—
treated as truths. This, I see for me and my development as
a self-sufficient woman who is really responsible for her
own happiness, is not a good thing. What are some of the
myths and old wives' tales I'm referring to, you ask? Let's

see. Here's one. Despite the fact that the women in the family are always praying and pulling together to make everyday life happen (like feeding the family, raising the family, nurturing the family), the minute a man sits down at the dinner table—regardless of who he is or where he has or has not been—some woman yells out, "Let the man bless the table!" What else? Oh. Here's a good one. All year long we women help each other, share child-raising responsibilities, heal one another when we are sick, shop for each other when we are weak, clean up after each other, provide companionship, support, laughter, and entertainment for each other — yes, we've got jokes! But once New Year's Eve rolls around—if you are a woman, you'd better not call or come over because if the first person to do so in the New Year is a woman, the house will have bad luck all year. Yeah. I know. I know. So, basically, a man, any man—the taxi driver, the bum off the street, somebody's loser boyfriend or abusive husband, the Negro who doesn't do anything for his kids and never will—can provide our entire home with good luck all year by just walking through the door or placing that first call in the New Year. But if my female self does it? Well, I wouldn't know because I would never be the one to let that happen. No matter what, I will not disrespect my grandmother's house in that way. I was raised better than that.

In my own home I have made a conscious decision to give that myth no power—if you are coming to my home with good intentions and blessings, man, woman, or child, you are welcome. My luck does not depend on you or your gender. My luck is between me and God, and you know what? Ever since I stopped personally practicing that New Year's Eve ritual, I have had unbelievable good luck!!

But I digress. You are getting my point, I think, about how these little things had to have affected me as a little girl and now, of course and unfortunately, as a grown woman.

Wait. There's more. Anytime anyone ever gets pregnant there is a verbal consensus among the matriarchs: I hope it's a boy! What else? Oh! If a man massages your head, your hair will grow. There is no criterion for this man, not a spiritual man, not an enlightened man, not even a man with clean, callus-free hands—just a man!!

Anyway. My truth is that I have a lot of ingrained ideas about men and women I have to rethink or else I will continue to give my power away in a relationship.

See. Now wasn't that fun! I've gone and inevitably made my grandma and aunties mad just so I can share my truths with you. I hope this has helped you to understand what I mean when I talk about listening to—and hearing—your truth. But if it hasn't, I have one more good one for you. One that doesn't have to do with my perception of men, one that I can't directly blame on my mother's family, one that is my issue and is all about me, and one that if I hadn't taken the time to really sit and listen to myself and look at my life, I would not have seen. One that once I realized it, I had to make a concerted effort to remedy immediately.

In my last relationship I was under a lot of stress with work and trying to find decent high schools for my daughter

and finances and . . . well, I was drinking too m[...]
Every chance I got. Until I fell fitfully asleep ea[...]
was a Level One relationship, so when it ended I took it in
stride. Still, I couldn't quite figure out what went wrong.
Then one sober night I had this thought: being drunk
around a guy is probably, maybe, for sure soooo not cute.
Or attractive.

Yeah. So there you have it. Happy now? Now it's your
turn. Here are just a few questions that if you answer them
honestly can help you find your truth. Take the time to reflect on your relationship. You will definitely see how you
could have done things differently, but most likely you will
realize that you were treated a certain way because on some
level you allowed it. C'mon. Be real. There is no one else but
you, your thoughts, and the resulting revelations. So think,
be still, and be truthful.

It's a painful process, but it's also liberating because in
your reflection and search for the truth about your relationship you just might discover certain truths. Maybe it wasn't
love after all. Maybe, just maybe, it was lust. Or maybe
even it was that other lethal *L* word—loneliness!!!

Yeah, you'd be surprised how many times we convince
ourselves we are in love but in fact we are just lonely. But the
realization of this is what is extremely freeing. Which is why
asking certain questions is essential, although I am aware
that I can't even begin to tap into your complicated psyche
or past pain by presenting you with the following series of
questions. Nor can I pretend that I can predict your progress.

My goal here is to present you with questions that will hopefully compel you to ask more intricate, introspective questions of yourself. Essentially, it's up to you to dig deeper. It's up to you to ask yourself the pertinent questions that will facilitate your self-awareness. So take your time and ask yourself these questions and answer them truthfully and to the best of your ability.

But the realization of your truths is extremely freeing.

✦   What are some ingrained, familial, and/or cultural beliefs you hold on to about relationships that you think need to be reassessed? *As I discovered, we are often affected by the ideas and ideologies held by people who are closest to us and/or people who came before us. We have things ingrained in us that we have come to accept, without asking ourselves if it is something that we actually agree with or want to abide by.*

✦   What is your personal definition of a good relationship? *Not everybody wants or needs the same things from his or her intimate relationships. You have to know what it is you want and need, what it is you are looking for from a relationship.*

✦   What is your personal definition of a bad relationship? *Only you know what you can and cannot handle in a relationship. Only you can decide what will and will not work for you.*

✦ According to your own definition, was your last relationship good or bad?

✦ Why did your last relationship end? *Sometimes endings are inevitable; sometimes they come out of nowhere. Sometimes the reasons relationships end are immediately clear; sometimes it takes time to figure out what really went wrong and why.*

✦ Who ended the relationship? Was it you or was it him? *Depending on who ended the relationship, you will discover a different set of emotions. If you ended it, you may feel liberated; if he ended it, you may feel abandoned. How do you feel?*

✦ If you ended it, are you happy with your decision? *At times we do things in the heat of the moment, in the throes of anger or passion, without really thinking them through. And sometimes we make a move that has been planned and calculated down to its final detail. Was your decision to end it spontaneous or did you really give it a lot of thought? Are you glad it's over or do you have lingering feelings of doubt? Do you want to reconcile?*

✦ If he ended it, how do you feel about his decision? *Sometimes you can be comfortable and content in a relationship, and then out of the blue the other person says it's over. Or you can both know the relationship is not working, but he was simply the one who had the courage to end it. Did you see this breakup coming? Were you blindsided or prepared? Are you okay with the decision or do you still have lingering feelings and hopes for reconciliation?*

✦   Are you having an easy time dealing with the end of the relationship? *When you know that something wasn't working or that the person really wasn't for you and vice versa, it's easy to let go.*

✦   Are you having a difficult time dealing with the end of the relationship? If so, why is it so hard for you to move on? *Usually when a relationship is really difficult to let go of, there is a serious lesson waiting to be learned. What is that lesson for you? If you are still holding on despite your efforts to the contrary, there is an unresolved issue you have with it. What are your unresolved issues with the relationship? Identify these issues so you can resolve them within yourself. It's no longer about him or what he did or didn't do. It's no longer about him and what he did or didn't say. It's about you, your actions, and your words.*

✦   In your last relationship, what did you learn about yourself that you like? *What are your good habits and beliefs that you bring to a relationship? Are you a good listener? Are you compassionate and patient? There are many things that you and only you have to offer in a relationship. Are you aware of what those things are?*

✦   In your last relationship, what did you learn about
    yourself that you do not like? *What are some things
    that you may need to address within yourself before mov-
    ing into your next relationship? Do you yell? Are you
    sloppy? Are you insensitive? Can you be callous?*

✦   Are you making an effort to address the things you've
    discovered about yourself that you do not particularly
    like? *Relationships are great opportunities to learn about
    ourselves via our interactions with others. If you've dis-
    covered something about yourself, your demeanor, your
    disposition, or your behavior that you really do not like,
    don't pass up the opportunity to address it, to change it.
    Make the most of an uncomfortable situation to better
    yourself and address your faults. If you don't do it now,
    they'll be back again, and again, and again. . . .*

✦   What are some of the things you did not like about
    your ex? *Oftentimes when there are things that bother us
    about others, they are really indications of things we
    don't like in ourselves.*

✦   What are some things that you like about yourself?
    *Are you funny? Do you have great legs? Are you well-
    read? A great cook? I identify, acknowledge, and cele-
    brate the great things about you. You don't have to wait
    for someone else to discover how wonderful you are. Try
    to constantly remind yourself of all your good points—
    even while working to overcome your faults. Make a*

concerted effort to actively and consistently do things that will enhance your assets.

✦   Referring to your most recent relationship—when you first met him, what was the first thing that ran through your mind? *Did you listen? Why or why not? Do you wish that you did listen or are you glad you didn't listen? Women have great survival instincts. Oftentimes we know upon a first meeting if someone is good for us. We pick up on little things, and we often don't acknowledge it. Think about your last relationship and see if there was any time when you listened to your instincts and when you did not.*

✦   What was your emotional state of mind when you entered your last relationship? *Were you happy and content with yourself and your life? Or were you insecure and seeking outside approval of your worth and importance?*

✦   Prior to your last relationship, how were you handling life's challenges and uncertainties on your own? *Were you tapping into your spiritual resources and reaching out to friends and family for emotional support in order to continue on your journey? Or were you looking for an escape? Did you need a distraction from your obligations and responsibilities? Or were you seeking someone to save you from yourself and rescue you from your life? Sometimes we use relationships as reasons not to follow our own paths and continue with our own plans.*

✦ Do you enjoy your own company? *Why? Why not? Some people simply don't like spending time alone. They may become bored or restless or, worse, despondent. But alone time is a part of life and something that you should try to embrace.*

✦ If you've discovered that you do indeed enjoy alone time, can you think of reasons why? *Maybe you were an only child and are used to being alone. Or maybe you are a child from a large family who cherished alone time. What are some things that you can think of that might account for your ability to spend time alone?*

✦ If you've discovered that you do not enjoy spending time alone, can you think of reasons why? *Maybe you are an only child who never got used to being alone. Or maybe you come from a large family and grew up with people around you all of the time and you find solitude unfamiliar and uncomfortable. What are some things that you can think of that might account for your inability to spend time alone?*

✦ Are you happy with your life's accomplishments? *As little girls we all have dreams about what we want to be when we grow up. Now that you are all grown up, have you realized any of your dreams? If so, what are they?*

✦ Do you still have unfulfilled goals and dreams? *If so, what are they? Are you doing anything at all to achieve*

*these goals and dreams? This is important because unful-
filled dreams lead to disappointment and frustration within
one's self. How can you be happy with someone else if
you are not happy with yourself?*

✦ Do you recognize a pattern with the men you date
and/or have relationships with? *What is the pattern?
For instance, are you only attracted to men who are already attached? Do you only go out with younger men?
Older men? Why? Do you find yourself dating the same
guy with a different face—a man who looks different
from your other boyfriends but who is exactly the same?
Why? What is it about this type that is attractive to
you? Do you think you need to change your patterns or
are you okay with them?*

✦ Do you only date men who can "do something" for
you—help you with your bills, advance your career,
etc.? *Why? Are you afraid to go it alone? Sometimes
women are not looking for love or companionship—they
are seeking a father figure, someone to take care of them.
Is this true of you? Why do you think that you can't
make it on your own?*

✦ Do you only date men whom you can "do something"
for? *Do you find that you are grooming, nurturing, providing for your men? Why? Do you like to feel needed?
Important? Necessary? Maybe you think that you have*

nothing else to offer. Or maybe you truly, simply enjoy doing these things. Just make sure you are doing them for the right reason—because you want to—not the wrong one—because you think you have to.

✦ Overall, do you think you make good or bad choices when it comes to relationships? *Think back to all the relationships you've had—from your first love to your last. In your opinion, was choosing to be with, spend time with, and share yourself with these people wise? Why or why not? If you feel you make wise decisions when it comes to men, what do you attribute this to? If you feel you make unwise decisions when it comes to men, what do you attribute this to?*

✦ Referring to your own definition, what was the best relationship you ever had? What made it so great? What was the worst relationship? What made it so bad? *Consider how your actions and attitudes may have contributed to both.*

✦ Are you fulfilled with your life the way it is right now? *If so, to what do you attribute this fulfillment? If not, what do you need to do in order for you to be fulfilled?*

Your Truth Shall Set You Free
By Kerika Fields

And then at some point
You see clearly
IT finally can be looked upon
For what it is
Has been
Will never be.
IT hurts
So good
So you cry
So much until
IT is enough
Then you smile
Triumphant
In the face of your truth
Because now you see
And you're finally free

NEWSFLASH: All these questions can be quite overwhelming! Don't get discouraged if you don't figure out everything right here, right now. Some things will be clear to you immediately; some things will take time to reveal themselves to you. Live your life, ask your questions, and listen for the answers. Know that these things take time. How long? Only time will tell. Heed the advice of the wise and wonderful Zora Neale Hurston, who said: "There are years that ask questions and years that answer." Know that no matter how long it does or doesn't take, your questions will be answered. That's the truth!

Chapter 6
RECIPES FOR RECOVERY

"I, woman, give birth: and this time to myself."
Alma Villanueva

The first step to recovering from a failed relationship is to acknowledge that you have been hurt. Your heart has been broken. If you break your ankle, are you going to go around walking on it? No, you're going to wrap it, soak it, and care for it until it is strong enough to support your body again. That is like your heart. How can you go back out into life putting your heart into your work, your creative projects, your family, your friends, your children, your new man, or your life when your heart is not healed, when it is still hurting? You can't. It can't be done. So now you have to sit down. Put your feet up and start to heal your heart.

But before I get to the serious stuff—the real hard heart, mind, body, and soul work that you must do to really recover—you need to know that there is another simple, easy step you can, should, and will inevitably take to begin the healing process. The next step—surprise!—is to cry. That's right. Let it all out. Don't be ashamed or afraid of your feelings. Find a quiet space—the bathroom, your bedroom—

139

where you can cry without the prying eyes and strained ears of children, family, friends, or coworkers. And don't worry, you will cry throughout your recovery process. At inappropriate times and in uncomfortable places, you will cry. But that's okay. You can't fight it anyway. Just remember to stick your Kleenex in your purse when you head out for work and be prepared to excuse yourself from the table at lunch when your song oh-so-conveniently comes from the random restaurant's loudspeakers. Oh, yes, my friend. It's going to be like that. The only way you are going to get over it is to go through it. Feel what you feel and don't fight it. C'mon. Nobody said love was easy. You take the good with the bad, and now that the good is over, the bad will be real bad. Bad nights when you can't sleep because you can't stop crying. Bad mornings with bad bags under your eyes because you barely slept a wink from crying all night.

The thing about the crying is, there is really nothing you can do about it, so why fight it? Crying is a necessary part of the healing process. In the beginning it will be exhausting and unbearable, but then it will die down as you begin to accept your situation and work through the recovery process. But be forewarned: just when you think you've evolved, when you're positive you've cried it all out, written it all out, prayed about it, asked yourself the hard questions, and maybe even feel you have forgiven him for breaking your heart or even forgiven yourself for letting your poor heart be broken (yes, we have to put some of the blame on ourselves), you'll be somewhere at some strange time in some stupid place and will not be able to fight the urge to cry. Trust me, I know. I was once on line at the bank and that damn song "Let's Just Kiss and Say Goodbye" came on the radio and I thought I was going to explode. There I was, waiting to deposit my tax-return check. I should've been happily making a mental list of the ways I was going to spend the much-needed money, yet I could not see two feet in front of me from the tears welling up in my eyes at the thought of a relationship I thought I'd long forgotten.

The bright side is that shedding tears is your body's way of cleansing itself, of releasing toxic emotions that if not discarded can cause disease in the body, a heavy heart, and a burdened soul. Think about it. When you feel a good cry coming on, right before the actual tears reach the corner of your eyes in preparation for their free fall, a warm ball of emotion forms in your chest right around your heart area. That feeling, this energy, rises up and out through your eyes through the tears you cry and through your mouth via the sobbing sounds and wails you make. But if you suppress this feeling in your chest, push it down, where does it go? It goes down into your body, your stomach, your womb. All this pain. All this poison. For your body's sake, you have to let it go, you have to let it out. So the tears that fall when you think of his eyes, his smile, the honeymoon, the wedding, the laughter, and the pain are actually a blessing, your anatomy's gift to you. I like to think that crying makes me look younger when it's all over, by washing all that past pain and anguish away and off of my face. So go ahead and cry—use those tears for what they're worth! You deserve to cry. Your heart has been broken. You have been hurt. Now it is time to heal.

But wait! Before you embark on your recovery plan, prior to hunkering down and doing the healing work, there is one thing you must do for you, and you must do it as soon as you can so you can get it out of your system. You must, and I reiterate must, throw yourself a pity party. Yeah, you read right! A good old-fashioned pity party where you can feel sorry for yourself, throw darts at his pictures, cry, complain, and all that. Get on the phone, call some of your closest friends, make some popcorn, pour some wine, pull out the Kleenex, and go for broke. This way the people you are closest to can hear your sob story, cry with you, and laugh with you, all on the comfort of your living-room couch. It will be fun and liberating. You get to be silly and sad simultaneously! The best benefit, though, is that you will have told everybody what happened, what went wrong, etc., etc., so you don't have to keep telling the Breakup Story over and over and over again. The next time they call and you are sounding sad—they will already know why. The next time they come over and you are looking a wreck—they will already know why. You won't have to keep pulling the bandage off the scar, showing it to everyone and saying, "See, see, see what happened," then slapping it clumsily back on. It will never heal that way. You have to expose it, let it be seen, and then cover it up until it is healed. Thus the pity party. Your people will know what you have been through (a bad breakup), know what you are about to go through (relationship recovery), and know what they need to do (be helpful and supportive or leave you alone!).

Did I mention that a pity party has two parts? Part A is the part where you pour your heart out to your friends like I mentioned previously. Part B is where you lie around and feel sorry for yourself by yourself. Each part should last only one evening, twenty-four hours at the most. They don't have to be one after the other or one before the other; they each just have to happen before you embark on your recovery journey. Now, for the pity party Part B, instead of calling up people, you will turn off your phone. You will order takeout, you will rent movies, you will place a box of Kleenex by your bed, you will put on your pajamas, you will climb into said bed, eat, watch movies, cry, laugh, feel sorry for yourself, doze in and out of consciousness, put on another movie, and do it again. With pity party Part B, you give yourself permission to be a bum for a day. No washing dishes. No watering the plants. No answering e-mails. No opening mail. It's just you, your chocolate mousse, your microwave meal, and your movies. Now, pity-party movies shouldn't be too sad or too romantic, but these elements *can* exist. There should probably be a handsome man somewhere on the screen at some point. The movie should be at least two hours long. The movie can be black and white, but if it is it must have excellent cinematography, and a good love scene can never be denied. Not sure what to rent? Try taking a look through *Cinematherapy for the Soul: The Girl's Guide to Finding In-*

spiration One Movie at a Time, by Nancy Peske and Beverly West. Or just pick one from my list—trust me, I have had my share of pity parties!

PITY-PARTY MOVIE PICKS

✦ *Claudine*—A young Diahann Carroll and a sexy James Earl Jones star as a man and woman trying to make love work in Chicago during the seventies despite a whole lot of kids and not a lot of money. The ultimate Black love story with a soundtrack by Gladys Knight and the late Curtis Mayfield. Trust me. You'll love it.

✦ *The Way We Were*—Pull out the tissues. A spunky Barbra Streisand and a handsome Robert Redford try to make it work but just can't seem to see eye to eye. And it's a shame, too. But hey, sometimes that's how it goes and you have to walk away and cherish your Memories (which is the tear-jerking song Ms. Streisand sings in this one).

✦ *Fried Green Tomatoes*—A story, set in the South, of a lifelong friendship between two women (Mary-Louise Parker and Mary Stuart Masterson) who are brought together after a shared family tragedy. The poignant story of female bonding and self-discovery revolves around a quirky murder mystery. You will be surprised when you find out who did it! Stars Kathy Bates and the late Jessica Tandy. With Cicely Tyson.

✦ *Thelma and Louise*—The ultimate road trip about two friends who are each unfulfilled in their lives. Thelma (Geena Davis), a bored housewife married to a brute of a man, and Louise (Susan Sarandon), a spunky waitress with a past, embark on a road trip that is funny, unfortunate, and sad. Still, it reiterates the idea that "you get what you settle for" in life. It also features a great cameo by a young, cute Brad Pitt, whose character serves as a reminder that just because a man looks good (well, in Brad's case, real good) doesn't mean he's not bad.

✦ *In America*—Sometimes it's the little independent movies that are the most moving, the most poignant. And *In America* is a fine example. It's about a small family who moves from Ireland to New York City in the early eighties so the father of the clan can pursue his acting dream during a time when rent in Manhattan was low and drug use and AIDS cases were high. Still, the movie, which is narrated by one of the two young daughters, is a beautiful love story about family, optimism, chasing your dreams, making new friends, and the importance of letting go of the past so you can live fully in the present. Plus, in 2003 Djimon Hounsou was nominated for a best supporting actor Oscar for his performance as the dying family friend who ends up being—literally—the family lifesaver. This movie is so good. And so is Mr. Hounsou's performance. You gotta check this one out.

✦ *Under the Tuscan Sun*—Diane Lane stars as a writer in California who discovers the husband she has been supporting has been having an affair instead of writing the next great American novel. After being convinced by her lawyer that it is in her best interest to sell the house to her ex-husband and his new family, she accepts an invitation to go to Italy from her lesbian friend (a cute cameo by *Grey's Anatomy* star Sandra Oh). But once she gets there, the unexpected and magical happens and her life is changed for the better forever. It's a nice movie and a great look at a woman taking a chance to start her life all over again on her own, and in a whole different country, no less!

✦ *Legends of the Fall*—Although the film is about the relationship among three brothers (Henry Thomas, Aidan Quinn, Brad Pitt), the subplot about the self-destructive dangers of being a woman in love with an unavailable man is riveting. Plus there's Brad Pitt on horseback, Brad Pitt in the water, Brad Pitt being bad, Brad Pitt being good. . . . Also stars Anthony Hopkins as the pioneering, antiwar father.

✦ *An Unmarried Woman*—This movie was released in theaters in 1978. So if some of the references and fashions are a little outdated, not to worry. Some situations stand the test of time. Jill Clayburgh stars as a woman from Manhattan's Upper East Side who is struggling to deal with her new identity and sexuality after her husband of sixteen years leaves her for a younger woman. Inevitably, she goes through a range of emotions, from anger to acceptance, but in the end? Well, you'll see.

✦ *Something's Gotta Give*—This movie is fun and funny and one of my favorites. Diane Keaton meets and falls in love with her daughter's boyfriend, who is played by Jack Nicholson. He's an old player who runs a hip-hop label and is not feeling her like she is feeling him. So she accepts the advances of a much younger, much finer man (Keanu Reeves) and throws herself back into her career as a playwright. That is, until Jack Nicholson comes to his senses.

✦ *Prime*—Uma Thurman falls for a younger man and unwittingly seeks support from a therapist who just happens to be her young lover's mother (Meryl Streep). The movie starts out as a situation comedy but ends up being a painful, truthful look at the emotional consequences of loving a younger man.

✦ *Bridget Jones's Diary*—This classic about the bumbling, bubbly Brit's adventures in drinking and dating is always fun. I think every woman can relate to it on some level. It also stars Hugh Grant as the horrible cad who betrays our Bridget, played wonderfully by Renée Zellweger.

✦ *Jerry Maguire*—Another one with Renée Zellweger, but this time her character is a single mom in love with a confused and career-challenged Tom Cruise. Still, when it's time to go with him she goes with her heart, and when it's time to walk away she lets him go. The scenes where the divorced-women's group meets at her sister's house (played by a pot-smoking Bonnie Hunt) are a riot. Regina King and Cuba Gooding Jr.'s appearance as an enviable couple in love make the movie worth seeing.

✦ *Rebecca*—Alfred Hitchcock's timeless story about a young secretary who marries a rich count, moves into his servant-run mansion, and finds herself intimidated by the memory and lingering presence of his dead wife is so good, so well-directed, so suspenseful. So see it. Joan Fontaine and Laurence Olivier star in the 1940 classic.

✦ *Casablanca*—This classic black-and-white romance about two war-torn lovers is romantic and intriguing. If you haven't seen it yet you should. It stars a gorgeous Ingrid Bergman and a gruff Humphrey Bogart.

✦ *Waiting to Exhale*—Whitney Houston, Angela Bassett, Loretta Devine, and Lela Rochon star in this, the ultimate women's movie. It's funny, it's sad, it's sexy, and it's all about the sisters. Plus, the soundtrack is slamming.

After you have had your pity party and all your self-loathing, laziness, and lethargy is out of your system, it's time to buckle down and start your relationship recovery. Let the healing begin!

THE PLAN

Our minds work best when there is order. This is why we have appointment books, BlackBerrys, and continually write "to-do lists." There are always so many things to get done during the day, it's more likely that we'll get some of it done if we write a list. And where would we be without schedules? Late or absent, that's where! So for this to work, you have to sit down and commit to a plan for your recovery. Since we are working with mind, body, and spirit, your schedule should be based on threes, depending on the level of your relationship. In addition to an explanation of each plan, I have provided a recommended time frame in which to carry it out. This does not mean that if you were in a Level Three relationship you will be all better at the end of three months. Not at all. Depending on you, your situation, and your emotions, you may need less time or more. I am in no way attempting to put a time frame on when your heartache should end, when you will be recovered from the relationship, because it is an ongoing process, an everyday struggle, a series of choices, a lifelong journey. The time frames suggested here represent the minimal time you should consciously set aside for yourself in your life for your recovery. Hopefully you will carry the things you learn about yourself and realize about the role you play in your relationships into your next relationship and ultimately utilize the information to fortify your relationship with yourself for the rest of your life.

Level One: Three-Day Recovery Plan
Level Two: Three-Week Recovery Plan
Level Three: Three-Month Recovery Plan

Take a moment to assess which one your relationship was. Whether it was Level One, Two, or Three, you'll still have work to do. It's easy to fall in love. It's hard to fall out.

TIME

Whichever time plan you choose to utilize, you must realize that healing from a hurtful relationship is really a lifelong process. At the end of the three days, three weeks, or three months, you are not going to just stop feeling what you're feeling. Hopefully, though, you will have developed a new perspective on the situation because you have given yourself some time for you. Just you. To think, to cry, to reassess, and to renew. And you will feel great. Like you can go back out there and do what you have to do in the world. So don't scoff at taking the time to "do you," love you, listen to you, and sort out your feelings. You have to get in touch with yourself and your emotions, and through this recovery regimen you can if only you will. These are the things you will need:

THE TOOLS

A journal (small enough to fit into your purse), a special mug, a juicer, a support group (friends and/or family members you are honest and open with), a prayer partner, an iPod/MP3 player, white candles, herbal teas of your choice (see chart below), essential oils (see chart on next page), a facial mask, lemons, purified/distilled water, sea salt or Epsom salts.

Herbal Teas

There are countless herbal teas to choose from, with various attributes and properties. By all means, have your favorite on hand. Below find some of my simple suggestions. Remember to sweeten with honey, maple syrup, or agave syrup. Or, even better, skip the sweetener. You're sweet enough anyway!

Herbal Tea	Benefits
Chamomile	Relaxes; purifies blood
Peppermint	Relaxes, refreshes; gentle laxative
Senna	Laxative
Red Raspberry	Tones, strengthens uterus
Echinacea	Boosts immune system
Dong Quai	Boosts energy (women's ginseng)
Saint-John's-wort	Antidepressant
Gotu Kola	Stimulates mind; improves memory

Essential Oils

Add a few drops to your bath, an oil burner, or natural body oil. Use sparingly and make sure it's the natural kind you find at a health food store. You only want the best for your skin!

Essential Oil	Properties
Eucalyptus	Opens pores, encourages creativity, and inspires change
Lavender	Cleanses aura, creates positive energy, relaxes muscles and senses
Rose	Fragrant, romantic, relaxing
Tea Tree	Acts as astringent, cleanses pores
Jasmine	Relaxes, supports self-love
Grapefruit	Energizes, makes you feel youthful, pretty, and powerful

THE ELEMENTS:
MIND, BODY, SPIRIT

When we love, we love for real. We love with all that we are, all that we have. So in order to heal our hearts, we have to use all that we have. We have to use our minds, bodies, and spirits. What's good for your body will be good for your spirit. By keeping a sharp mind, you will remember to care for your body. By staying in touch with your spirit, you will refuse to neglect your body and mind. You get it. It's all interrelated.

Mind

You are going to get through this. You will be all right.
You will be happy again. You will recover. At first you may
not think this is the case. Initially, you may be so devastated
that the thought of going on with your life, of living without
the man you so loved (or thought you loved), can seem unbearable. But even through the tears and the tirades, something in you knows that this too shall pass.

The strength of your mind will determine the speed of
your recovery. Once you have accepted the fact that the relationship is over, you can begin to take the necessary steps.
But you *have* to make up your mind. You *will* avoid the Abyss.
You *will* get over this. And then once you make up your mind,
you have to keep it there, focused on your decision and your
goal, which, by the way, is to heal your broken heart the
healthy way. I must emphasize the importance of this step,
of making up your mind, of deciding that you will recover,
of deciding that, yes, you will survive this. When people are
victims of debilitating accidents or life-threatening diseases—
things that can lead to years of recovery via physical therapy
and various medical procedures—they have to, at some point,
decide to recover or else they never will. They have to mentally gird themselves against all the inevitable setbacks, pain,
and frustrations that will come with their healing process
and decide to actually do it—to move past the pain, try their
best, give it their all, commit to the program—so that they
can eventually reclaim their lives. So, yes, make up your

mind! It is your mind that is going to weed out unwanted thoughts like "I'll never meet someone else" that can lead to unwanted actions like trying to get him back when you know he's no good for you anyway. To keep your mind strong, you will need tools. The tools of prayer, fasting, cleansing, reading, affirmations, exercise, laughter, tears, meditation, massage. At the end of your self-appointed re-covery time, you will be a better person for having taken time for yourself. During this self-imposed sabbatical, this is your time. That does not mean that you stop taking care of your responsibilities or that you cut yourself off from the world (though at times you will have to—it's required!). It just means you are mindful of You. You are taking care of You. You are loving you and falling in love with yourself all over again. You have been so busy reaching for and trying to hold on to your man that you lost a grip on yourself. It's time to get a grip, literally and figuratively. Some of the things that are required are challenging, of course, but it's worth it.

Relationship Recovery Journal

Here you will write down all thoughts pertaining to your relationship—the good, the bad, and the ugly. Journaling is imperative to your recovery because you can get your emo-tions and frustrations out and onto the page. The best part is that you can always go back to your entries and remind yourself of your feelings and revelations so that when you are feeling weak you can be reinforced by your own words. You don't have to spell correctly or use your perfect handwriting. You just have to put your feelings, realizations, and affirmations down on paper so you can read them over and remind yourself of what you are going through. So you are going to create and utilize a Recovery Journal. Any blank-paged book will do, but the smaller the better—it should be able to fit into your everyday purse so that when you get inspired or frustrated or confused you can put your feelings and lamentations on paper. You can and should journal anywhere—on the subway, during a solo lunch, at a local coffee shop while waiting for a client. But the best place is at home in your bathroom or bedroom sanctuary after a long day while sipping a cup of warm herbal tea. Regardless of when or where you write in your journal, there is one thing you must write. It is a love letter to you, a Self-Love Letter.

Copy the following, freehand, into your journal. You can add more or make changes to suit you; just make sure you fortify yourself and your spirit with words of support and encouragement, with words you know your heart needs to hear. (This should be the first page in your Recovery Journal.)

Date_____
I love you, [your name]_____. You are so beautiful,
special, sweet, and sensitive. But you are hurt right now.
Your heart has been broken and you are in pain. That's
okay. Because I'm going to take care of you, honey. I'm
going to bathe you and oil you and massage you—your
face, neck, legs, feet, hands, and thighs. And I'm going

to feed you like the Queen that you are. That's right. Only the best foods—fresh fruits and vegetables, pure water, nuts, grains, juices, and delicious and diverse herbal teas—for you and your special self. I'm going to take care of you, boo. I'm going to let you rest. I'm going to allow you to cry. It's going to be all right. Because I'm here and I love you. I love you always. I love you actively. I love you unconditionally.

Sincerely,
Self

Once you have written your Self-Love Letter, you can write your Let-Go Letter. The Let-Go Letter is written to the person you are letting go of—but not to worry. You will not have to give it to him. In fact, you shouldn't give it to him, because although it's about him, it's only for you. It's for you to address that you are letting go of the relationship, that you are moving on. In the letter you can forgive him for any wrongdoings and forgive yourself for the same. You can vent your rage or confess your everlasting love. You can put all your unresolved emotions and feelings in the letter. Then fold it up, rip it up, throw it away, and let it go.

Now, let the journey, via journaling, begin. From this point on, every day you will write in your journal. You can write whatever you want; it can be pages and pages or just a thought, a quote, a joke. Something. Some words, putting the pen to paper about the process you are going through. The only real rule or requirement is that you address on a daily basis the following question: "What did I do to love myself today?" Since you've made up your mind to love yourself, you must remember this: "love" is an action word. So to really love yourself, you have to take action, you have to do something, so do something special, something simple, to show yourself that you do love yourself. This is especially crucial if you feel like you don't love yourself due to various personal situations and/or circumstances. By doing something specifically for you—taking an exercise class, getting a facial, saying a prayer, going to a great party, soaking your feet, buying a great-fitting dress you need (and can afford), enjoying a delicious and healthy meal—you are loving yourself. The term is overused, I know. It seems that everyone's solution to everything these days is "Love yourself, girl." It seems like that's the advice people always give. But do you know why? Because loving you is crucial. Loving yourself—unconditionally, whether you're weak and strong, fat or skinny, broke or banking—should be something you do all the time. Unfortunately, I really don't think a lot of us know what loving self really means, nor do we really comprehend the practicality of self-love. It was hard for me, too. It took me some time to get it, but eventually and thankfully the truth behind the concept became so clear.

When you love your man, your mother, your children, and your friends, you are concerned with their health and well-being. You are concerned if something is wrong with one of them, if something isn't right. You want them healthy, strong, thriving. So you cook their favorite meal, or make that trip to the supermarket when they can't, or stay up studying with them all night so they pass that test so they get the job they want or accepted to the school of their choice. You do whatever you can to be supportive. They like grape juice? You try to keep it in the house. Prune juice good for daddy's system? You pick some up before you swing by each Saturday, even keep your eye out for sales. You go to the hospital when they are sick and celebrate with them when they are well. You always want to see them thriving, growing, shining. And you *do* whatever you can to facilitate and even ensure their happiness. Why? Because you *love* them. Now, take all that energy, focus, caring, concern, and compassion and turn it around. Look at yourself. Look at your life. Are you *loving* yourself? Doing what's best for you? Bettering yourself through school? Fulfilling your potential? Are *you* taking *your* vitamins, keeping *your* doctor's appointments, getting *your* rest? That's what loving yourself is. *Doing* what is best for you. *Doing* it consistently. *Doing* it every day of your life. So during your recovery, you will take an active assessment of if, when, and how you are actively loving yourself by asking yourself every day one simple but pertinent question: "What did I do to love myself today?"

Some days will be great, as in "Today I went to the gym and treated myself to a massage" or "Today I made a fresh salad" or even "Today I finally broke out the juicer and made some fresh juice." But some days you will be reaching, as in "Today I drank a glass of water." But no matter. You *will* find something, because every day we do something to love ourselves or we would not be here, living and breathing, even something as simple as "Today I washed my face" or "Today I took ten deep breaths." Some days, depending on your state of despair or depression, washing your face, brushing your teeth, and drinking some water might be all the self-love you can muster up, but no matter. This exercise will help in at least two ways. First of all, knowing that at the end of the day you have to write about what you did to love yourself that day will make you more prone to do something loving (so you can have something to report back to your journal). Secondly, and mainly, you will begin to see that the little things do count, that no matter how bad you feel, you do love yourself, because of the little things you do. No matter how little—like taking a vitamin, choosing water over soda at lunch, smoking one cigarette instead of the two you wanted—it all adds up and it all counts. That's right. I know we all have addictions, issues, insecurities, and doubts. We've all made mistakes, had mis-judgments and done things we regret. These things cannot be your focus, and they won't be because every evening, even if it's only five minutes, you will write what you did to love yourself that day and you will begin to see that a little goes a long way, and the self-loving acts will get bigger and bigger as time goes by.

If you truly find this task to be too daunting, I've tried to make it easier for you by creating a Daily Self-Love Check-list. You can actually make a copy of it and staple it into your journal. Or put it on your refrigerator. Or stick it to your mirror. Whatever. Just stick to it! (For a printer-friendly version of the Daily Self-Love Checklist, visit hesgone youreback.com.)

Daily Self-Love Checklist

Name: _____   Week Beginning: _____

ACTIVITY	Sun.	Mon.	Tues.	Wed.	Thurs.	Fri.	Sat.	Comments
Exercise								
Run/Walk								
Stretches								
Yoga								
Pilates								
Bike Ride								
Dance Class								
Aerobics Class								
Peace Bath								
Enema								
Fast								
A Talk Fast								
Facial								
Manicure								
Pedicure								
Massage								

ACTIVITY	Sun.	Mon.	Tues.	Wed.	Thurs.	Fri.	Sat.	Comments
Self-Massage								
Feet								
Hands								
Face								
Abdomen								
Fresh Fruit								
Vegetables/Salad								
Sugar-Free Juice								
Herbal Tea								
Water								
Prayer								
Meditation								
Visualization								
Affirmation								
Journal Entry								
Afternoon Nap								
Other*								

* *Weight Watchers meeting, prayer group, church service, self-help seminar, AA or NA meeting, etc.*

Affirmations: I have provided you a few *affirmations*, but I think it will be better if you write your own. Put your name in them. Personalize them. Address your own individual issues in your affirmations. If you need to be more confident, more assertive, more positive, write affirmations that reinforce the truth you can and will be all that you need to be. Write these affirmations in your journal. In fact, your own affirmations should be recorded in your Recovery Journal so when you need to read them you know exactly where they are. You should say your affirmations aloud daily for best results. The spoken word is a powerful thing. After all, "In the beginning was the Word." It all starts there. So when creating your affirmations, choose words of power, use words of love and positivity, because as you write them and say them you will be creating your own life's reality. Even if, at the moment, you don't believe it, write it and say it anyway. It will be your affirmations—in addition to your prayers—that you will go to and use when your mind is going to a dark place, a mad place, and a sad place. It will be affirmations that lead you back to yourself and the truth about yourself.

Some Suggestions

I am healing.
I will survive this.
I love myself.
I am loved.
I am love.

I attract only positive people into my life.

I am worthy of a committed, trusting relationship.

I deserve the best.

I am the best.

I am beautiful on the inside and on the outside.

I am unique—one of a kind.

I am divine.

Of all the affirmations you create and/or discover, there is one that is the most important, the most powerful, and the most common. What is it? It is this: I love you. Try it. Tell yourself, "I love you." We say it all the time to everyone—our kids, our friends, our lovers—but we rarely consciously, actively say it to ourselves. And it is so simple. And it is so powerful. And it is so necessary. I love you. Say it again. I love you. Even though I am not perfect, I love you. Even though I make mistakes, I love you. Even when you are tired and confused and upset, I love you. Say it whenever you can. Say it in the morning. Say it at night. Say it on the train or while driving your car. Put your name behind it and make it your mantra. Trust me, it works and it feels so good. *I love you, Kerika. I love you. I love you. I love you.*

Books

During your time to yourself, take advantage by indulging in some good books. You might want to reach for your novel when you just want to get into someone else's world or drama, your journal when you want to write down your feelings, and your nonfiction books when you want to be inspired in all aspects of your life. But you will also need some real, true spiritual reading. Regardless of your religion, you can find strength and inspiration from books of scripture like the Bible, the Quran, or the Bhagavad Gita. Along with these, take this time to read some self-help books that will assist your growth and transition. There are many books out there that can be helpful to your recovery. I'm sure you are fond of a few and have friends who can make suggestions. Either way, I've provided you with a brief list of books I like and that were instrumental in my recovery. I recommend you take a look at the list, pick out a few books you think you will like, and have them on hand. Because, trust me, you will stop crying, you will stop obsessing about him on the phone, you will stop sleeping every chance you get—and when you do, you will need some good books at your disposal. There's no better way to keep you mind off of your misery than by reading things that will help you create and maintain a fulfilling future. In other words, there's never been a better time to hit the bookstore, or better yet, the library!

RECOVERY READING LIST

Heal Thyself: For Health and Longevity, by Queen Afua
Sacred Woman: A Guide to Healing the Feminine Body, Mind, and Spirit, by Queen Afua
Imagine a Woman in Love with Herself: Embracing Your Wisdom and Wholeness, by Patricia Lynn Reilly

The Value in the Valley: A Black Woman's Guide through Life's Dilemmas, by Iyanla Vanzant

Yesterday, I Cried: Celebrating the Lessons of Living and Loving, by Iyanla Vanzant

Something More: Excavating Your Authentic Self, by Sarah Ban Breathnach

Simple Abundance: Living by Your Own Lights, by Sarah Ban Breathnach

The Wonders of Solitude, edited by Dale Salwak

The Game of Life and How to Play It, by Florence Scovel Shinn

Sensual Celibacy: The Sexy Woman's Guide to Using Abstinence for Recharging Your Spirit, Discovering Your Passions, Achieving Greater Intimacy in Your Next Relationship, by Donna Marie Williams

On My Own: The Art of Being a Woman Alone, by Florence Falk

Sex for One: The Joy of Selfloving, by Betty Dobson, PhD

The Thrill of the Chaste: Finding Fulfillment While Keeping Your Clothes On, by Dawn Eden

You Can Heal Your Life, by Louise Hay

Women's Bodies, Women's Wisdom: Creating Physical and Emotional Health and Healing, by Christiane Northrup, MD

The Four Agreements: A Practical Guide to Personal Freedom, A Toltec Wisdom Book, by Don Miguel Ruiz

The Seat of the Soul, by Gary Zukav

The Path to Love: Spiritual Strategies for Healing, by Deepak Chopra

Sassy, Single, and Satisfied: Secrets to Loving the Life You're Living, by Michelle McKinney Hammond

How to Avoid the 10 Mistakes Single Women Make, by Michele McKinney Hammond

The Positive Bible from Genesis to Revelation: Scripture That Inspires, Nurtures, and Heals, compiled by Kenneth Winston Caine

Choosing Truth: Living an Authentic Life, by Harriette Cole

In the Spirit, by Susan L. Taylor

The Transformative Power of Crisis: Our Journey to Psychological Healing and Spiritual Awakening, by Robert M. Alter with Jane Alter

Chicken Soup for the African American Woman's Soul, by Jack Canfield, Mark Victor Hansen, and Lisa Nichols

Souls Revealed: A Souls of My Sisters Book of Revelations and Tools for Healing Your Spirit, Soul, and Life, by Dawn Marie Daniels and Candace Sandy

10 Good Choices That Empower Black Women's Lives, by Grace Cornish

Women & Money: Owning the Power to Control Your Destiny, by Suze Orman

Can I Get a Witness?: Black Women and Depression, by Julia A. Boyd

A Call to Fast: Taking the Spiritual Journey, by Fay Andrea Daley

When Things Fall Apart: Heart Advice for Difficult Times, by Pema Chödrön

Body

Exercise

The best way to start to recover is to start to really care for your body. It is, after all, your temple! At this point, your body is filled with old pain and memories: stagnant energy. You must get moving. As discussed previously, studies have shown that exercise produces endorphins and endorphins prevent you from serious depression. And remember, you must avoid the Abyss at all costs. So get going. You may not feel all that great about yourself right now and the thought of going into a room full of people and jumping around at a gym may not be appealing or financially feasible. No excuse. A walk around the block or through the park is free and priceless to your body, as it will help clear your mind and enrich your spirit while invigorating your body and helping you to lose and/or maintain your weight (depending on the food choices you've been making). I highly recommend using this time to try something new. If you always go to the gym, start jogging in the park. If you jog, take kickboxing. If you've never been to the gym, join one now. If you're an aerobics girl—loving the loud music and fun steps—take a quiet, relaxing yoga class. If all you ever do is yoga, take a boot camp. Mix it up. Try something different from your normal routine. This will help you get a different perspective on things. Whatever you do is up to you, but DO SOMETHING. Staying active is important in keeping your head in the right place. Besides, you're going to need something to do with all that extra energy you're not putting into him. So look into doing something new as long as it's something physical.

I highly recommend yoga and Pilates. Yoga deals with balance, and staying on balance is always a good thing. Not to mention how well it tones your body. And Pilates is based on strengthening your core. So you basically have to be balanced and centered in these classes. And since most yoga and Pilates classes are ninety minutes long, that's a guaranteed hour and a half that you won't be thinking about your ex! The best part about yoga and Pilate's classes is that you literally can't think about your problems. Once I was in a Bikram yoga class and let my mind wander out of the room, away from the moment to a time and place with someone long gone, and I actually fell backward. On my butt. In one of my favorite and oft-practiced poses! I had to focus. I had to be in the moment. I had to admit, I was glad I was in a class doing something for myself instead of feeling sorry for myself.

Peace Bath

Have you ever taken a Peace Bath? They are great to relax you and soothe your muscles after exercising, and they are easy to do. Just run your tub with warm to hot water, add Epsom salts, brew a cup of relaxing herbal tea, maybe put on some relaxing jazz music, light a candle, and get in. A Peace Bath should be a staple in your recovery. A Peace Bath is a beautiful thing. Embrace it. Personalize the ritual with your own special touches—your favorite aromatic candle or instrumental CD. Prior to getting into your Peace Bath, pray for release and freedom. Ask God to help you let go. When you get out of your Peace Bath you will feel relaxed, lighter, and at peace. The Epsom salts and herbal tea will help pull toxins from your body, the candles and music will help you clear your mind, and the prayer will rejuvenate your spirit. Make the time to really enjoy your bath— possibly after everyone in the house has gone to bed, or when you know you can really relax and don't have to rush out the door to work or a meeting. The best time to have a Peace Bath is at night, right before bedtime. It can help melt away the stress of your day. It can help you sleep better. It can do wonders for your body, mind, and spirit. May the Peace Bath be with you!

Self-Love Spa

I know how wonderful and relaxing going to a spa can be. There is nothing like being pampered, taken care of, and massaged. There's nothing like having your body scrubbed from head to toe, or being given a facial treatment that opens your pores and makes your skin glow. It's a wonderful luxury that every woman should indulge in when she can. Unfortunately, time constraints and/or financial limitations make it impossible for most of us to visit a spa and have these great treatments on a regular basis. Still. That can't and shouldn't stop us from finding creative ways to take care of ourselves or pamper ourselves. After discovering how wonderful a Peace Bath can be, you may be inspired to turn your bathroom into your very own at-home Self-Love Spa! I do hope so! I hope you use the space and take the time to pamper yourself in your own home, with your own resources, at your own leisure. I know I do! I know I don't always have the time or money to spend at a spa. So I've created little beautifying things I can always do at home to make myself feel good, to take care of myself, to pamper myself. Here are a few of my favorites:

∾ *Refreshing Foot Soak*

Epsom salt

Peppermint soap

Eucalyptus or peppermint oil

Grape-seed oil

Lotion

Clean socks

Pumice stone

Fill a basin or foot spa with hot water. Add Epsom salt and peppermint soap. Place your feet in the basin and let sit/soak for at least ten minutes. After ten minutes, use a natural pumice stone to rub heels, calluses, and corns. Dry feet with a towel. Place a few drops of peppermint oil or eucalyptus oil into some grape-seed oil. Rub feet thoroughly. Give yourself a mini foot massage. Slather a rich, creamy lotion on feet. Place feet into clean cotton socks. Put your feet up and smile!

∿ *Beautiful Body Scrub*

½ cup sea salt
1 cup olive oil
¼ cup grape-seed oil

Fill a glass bowl or jar with sea salt. Add olive oil and grape-seed oil. Mix together until the salt has absorbed the oil. Use the body scrub after a Peace Bath or a shower. While standing in shower, rub salt scrub all over your clean body. Pay special attention to elbows, knees, and heels. Use your hand to make brisk circular motions. Rinse off with warm water. Pat yourself dry with a towel. Your skin will feel so smooth!

∿ *Avocado Mask*

½ ripe avocado
1 teaspoon fresh lemon juice

Mush avocado meat into bowl and add lemon juice. Place mixture in refrigerator while you wash your face and neck with mild soap. Pat your face dry, remove mixture from refrigerator, and slather on your face. Leave on for twenty minutes. Rinse thoroughly. Let your skin breathe for another half hour, and then apply a rich facial moisturizer. (Great for women with dry skin!)

✑ *Lemon/Aloe Facial*

½ lemon
1 slice ripe aloe plant
1 pot water
1 clean towel

*Bring water to boil. Remove from heat. Let it sit to cool as
you wash your face thoroughly with mild soap. Pat dry with
towel. Use towel to create a "tent" to place over your head.
Stand over the water for about three minutes, letting the steam
engulf your face and open your pores. Pat face dry again and
rub lemon all over your face. This may burn a little! Let stand
for a few minutes or for as long as you can stand it! Splash face
with cold water until all lemon is off. Slice open aloe to jelly.
Rub aloe jelly all over your face. Let sit overnight. Rinse off
aloe in the morning. (Great for women with oily skin!)*

These are several of my at-home spa remedies. For more or to
share some of yours with me, visit hesgoneyoureback.com.

Alternative Health Practices

In addition to exercise, Peace Baths, and at-home spas,
there are other ways to get your body back in balance, to center your energy. These options may be unfamiliar to you, but
they have been proven to heal body, mind, and spirit. If you
have the inclination or the resources, why not give them a try?

Acupuncture: Acupuncture is a form of Oriental medicine that focuses on balancing energy in the body, mind,

and spirit simultaneously. According to Western medicine, the effects of acupuncture are probably the result of stimulating the nervous system to release chemicals that may in turn release other hormones, producing the desired effects. This theory is supported by the basic research work that has shown acupuncture's effect on insulin, thyroid hormones, growth-stimulating hormone, beta-endorphin, white-blood-cell production, and plasma cholesterol levels. In traditional Chinese medicine training, acupuncture is believed to modulate the flow of energy (Qi) in its channels, or meridians, to restore balance. How does it work? Small, thin needles are placed in "acupressure points"—points on energy meridians that correspond to different organs in the body. Acupuncture has been used for various ailments including chronic pain, addiction, and cosmetic purposes (certain meridians are targeted to relax the muscles in the face, resulting in a more youthful appearance).

Reiki: This is a Japanese technique for stress reduction and relaxation that also promotes healing. It is administered by "laying on hands" and is based on the idea that an unseen "life-force energy" flows through us and is what causes us to be alive. If our "life-force energy" is low, then we are more likely to get sick or feel stress, and if it is high, we are more capable of being happy and healthy. The word "Reiki" is made of two Japanese words—"Rei," which means "God's Wisdom or the Higher Power," and "Ki," which is "life-force energy." So Reiki is actually "spiritually guided life-force energy." In my experience, Reiki is great when you're feeling a little off or anxious and you just don't know why. It helps to bring your energy back into your body. I actually have a friend who was studying the technique and allowed me to be his guinea pig. I happily obliged and was pleasantly surprised at the immediate effects of this ancient technique.

Yoga: I know I refer to yoga a lot, but that's because I love it. For me it's a great way to stretch my body, get my heart pumping, and my blood flowing without having to jump up and down or run all over the place. It helps me be calm, if only for ninety minutes. But there are many different types of yoga to explore.

✦ **Vinyasana yoga**—This type of yoga is all about movement. Whereas other forms of yoga deal with getting into poses and holding them for a set time, Vinyasana is all about flow. It's all about diversity, too, which means depending on the instructor, your class can differ regarding the pace and which poses are included. Most times, you can count on these four being somewhere in the mix: Downward Facing Dog (you are on your hands and feet with your midsection in the air); Plank Pose (you flow from the former position to a straight—or plank—position); Chaturanga (from Plank, your arms bend back, your upper arms hug into your sides. You lower down toward the floor, stopping when your forearms and upper arms are at a right angle. Keeping the whole body very level, you push back into your heels); Upward Facing Dog (an intense backbend. You keep the legs engaged and off of the floor, while pressing the tops of the feet down and dropping the hips).

✦ **Hatha yoga**—Hatha yoga is the most commonly practiced style of yoga in the United States today. The word "hatha" is derived from the Indian words for "sun" (*ha*) and "moon" (*tha*), which is why this style is often referred to as the yoga of "opposite pairs." Hatha yoga differs from other styles of yoga in that it focuses more on breathing and poses than on meditation. In group-fitness classes that teach hatha, yoga instructors usually begin by practicing pranayama, deep breathing through the nose. They lead the class through a series of about ten asanas (postures) and end with three to five minutes of quiet meditation.

✦ **Kundalini yoga**—Most techniques include the following features: cross-legged positions; the positioning of the spine (usually straight); different methods to control the breath; the use of mantras, closed eyes, and mental focus (often on the sound of the breath). Kundalini yoga links movement with breath. It is differentiated by a direct focus on moving energy through the chakra system, stimulating the energy in the lower chakras and moving it to the higher chakras. The chakras are energy centers, seven in total, located beginning at the base of the spine and ending at the top of the head. An eighth chakra exists in Kundalini yoga, which is the electromagnetic field, sometimes called "aura." The aura is thought to be strengthened through the practice of Kundalini yoga. Kundalini yoga is sometimes called "the Yoga of Awareness."

✦ **Bikram yoga**—This yoga is a series of twenty-six postures performed in a hot (over one hundred–degree) room in an effort to create a climate that is conducive to where the yoga was originated (in crazy-hot India). The heat helps with detoxifying the body and improving flexibility. This yoga is great for toning the body and keeping the mind clear and focused. It can get intense, but if you like heat you'll eventually get used to it. Personally, I love to sweat and I love this practice because no matter where I go in any part of the world, regardless of the instructor, I know I will be practicing the same exact twenty-six poses in the same exact sequence. And for all my affinity for the unpredictable, sometimes I just need to know exactly what I'm getting myself into.

Massage Therapy: Like yoga, there are very many different types of massage techniques to choose from. Her are a few of the most common:

✦ **Swedish massage**—This is the most common type of massage therapy in the United States even though it was developed in—you guessed it—Sweden. Massage therapists use long, smooth strokes, kneading, and circular movements on superficial layers of muscle using massage lotion or oil. Swedish massage therapy can be very gentle and relaxing. If you've never had massage before, this is a good place to start.

✦ **Aromatherapy massage**—Aromatherapy massage is massage therapy with the addition of one or more scented plant oils called essential oils to address specific needs. The massage therapist can select oils that are relaxing, energizing, stress reducing, balancing, etc. If you are dealing with an injury that is of an emotional nature, this might be the type of massage to try.

✦ **Deep tissue massage**—Tight calves? Wiry neck muscles? Sore from exercising? This massage targets the deeper layers of muscle and connective tissue, which is why, sometimes, you can be sore for up to two days after a treatment.

✦ **Shiatsu**—Shiatsu is a form of Japanese bodywork that uses localized finger pressure in a rhythmic sequence on acupuncture meridians. Each point is held for a few seconds to improve the flow of energy and help the body regain balance. People are normally pleasantly surprised when they try shiatsu for the first time. It is relaxing, yet the pressure is firm, and there is usually no soreness afterward.

✦ **Reflexology**—Although reflexology is sometimes called foot massage, it is more than simple foot massage. Reflexology involves applying pressure to certain points on the foot that correspond to organs and systems in the body. Reflexology is very relaxing, especially for people who stand on their feet all day or just have tired, achy feet. This is a great one to try after a night out on the town in six-inch heels.

Food: We all know that food can be comforting. So, during your recovery process, you must not forget the ugly truth—food can also be lethal. It's very important that you make the right food choices. Too much sugar, alcohol, salt, fried foods, and processed foods will make you overemotional, moody, depressed, and bloated. And since you're already brokenhearted, a little jaded, and plenty confused, who needs all of that? Not you. Not now. Not ever. Once you are aware of this, you can make better food choices. So instead of curling up with a bowl of ice cream, how about a bowl of grapes? Or a slice of watermelon? Craving comfort food (read: carbs!!!) like mashed potatoes or pasta? How about a fabulous salad with all your favorite toppings like cucumber, tomatoes, carrots, baby corn . . . ? You get the point. You'll enjoy it more if you know it's good for you. More importantly, keep in mind that the number-one killer of women is heart disease. This can be due to our stressful lives and the way we deal with our emotions—did someone say suppression?—but probably the biggest cause is a heavy diet rich in cholesterol, fat, and salt. We have to make better choices—it really is a matter of life and death. On the next page is a chart of healthy foods and the benefits they provide for you. Hopefully this will inspire you to make healthy food choices that will support and promote your healing.

Healthy Fruits and Vegetables

Food	Postive Properties
Apples	Protects your heart, prevents constipation, cushions joints
Beets	Protects your heart, controls blood pressure, aids weight loss
Blueberries	Protects your heart, combats cancer, stabilizes blood sugar
Cherries	Protects your heart, alleviates insomnia, slows aging process
Grapes	Protects your heart, enhances blood flow, alleviates kidney stones
Strawberries	Protects your heart, calms stress, boosts memory
Sweet potatoes	Lifts mood, strengthens bones, nourishes womb
Watermelon	Prevents constipation, stabilizes blood sugar, hydrates body
Lemons	High in vitamin C; cleanses blood

Cleansing Diet: I know Frank Sinatra sang a song about it, but people can really get under your skin!! Their scent, their saliva, their sperm, their favorite food. Yes, I said sperm. If, in your relationship, you were sexually active and

not using condoms, most likely at some point during intercourse his sperm entered your body in one way or another.
Sperm is a protein-packed substance that can be at times
toxic. Especially if your partner was a heavy meat eater, a
drinker, or a smoker—his sperm could have been full of poi-
sons and toxins that went right into you know where. And
your bloodstream. All this you have been sharing, and now
that your relationship is over your body is literally going
through withdrawal. Help it along with a cleansing diet. It
doesn't have to be anything drastic; it can be as simple as
adding a salad to your plate and staying away from foods
that obviously clog you up like bread, pasta, cheese, and
meat. The objective here is to help your body release the
negative emotions and various toxins that have inevitably
been stored in your body from fighting, crying, taking too
many sleeping pills, eating the wrong foods, having unpro-
tected sex, and neglecting yourself. If you're up to it, this
would be a great time to consider doing a fast. There are
many ways to fast and many books and authors that claim
theirs is the best. There's the vegetable-juice fast, the
lemon-water fast, the grapefruit fast, the live-food fast, and
so on and so forth. If you look on the Internet you will be
bombarded with various forms of fasting that tout various
benefits, from clear skin to more energy to weight loss.

I will not pretend I can predict the benefits of fasting. I can
only tell you from personal experience that fasting has been
beneficial to me because when I clean out my body, my mind
works better. I am more creative and optimistic. And I pray
more (as in "Lord, please don't let me eat that cookie!").

Which is an interesting element of fasting that makes it very different from dieting. Dieting is only about losing weight, but fasting has a spiritual element. After all, Jesus fasted for forty days and nights way back in the day. Today, though, people fast to eliminate toxins from the body, which may be a necessary part of life in these toxic times. This is probably why there are so many books and Web sites and retreats dedicated to fasting. Of all the information I have encountered, I've found that the most useful and comprehensive information on fasting—especially when it comes to women and our unique needs, challenges, and goals—is Queen Afua's classic, timeless *Heal Thyself* (see the Recovery Reading List).

Fasts are recommended during times of crisis—physical crises, emotional crises, financial crises. Fasts are done when you don't know what else to do, so you just stop. Sit. Be still. Pray. Fast. Let your body clean out and let your mind get clear. Which is why postbreakup is the perfect time to do a fast. Confused much? Emotional a lot? Discombobulated? Did you ever stop to think that it could be your diet—all the sugar and caffeine we consume daily—that could be throwing you into a tailspin? A fast might be just what the doctor ordered. But fasting can be complicated and some say harmful to your overall health by depriving you of certain essential nutrients. It is also debatable whether the body stores certain nutrients in its fat cells and fasting for a short period of time will not harm you and could be helpful. So instead of a fast (which indicates deprivation) I propose a "Live-Food Feast," which is—you can basically eat whatever you want as long as it's alive!

Eliminate:

Sugar	Red meat
Caffeine	Chicken
Alcohol	Fish
Dairy (milk, eggs, cheese, butter, etc.)	

It sounds challenging, but don't think about what you cannot have. Focus on what you can have:

Vegetables:

Artichokes	Kale
Broccoli	Okra
Cauliflower	Asparagus
Beets	Zucchini
Sweet potatoes	Squash
Dandelion greens	Pumpkin
Mustard greens	Mushrooms
Collard greens	Cabbage
Spinach	

Fruit:

Cucumbers	Oranges
Watermelon	Tangerines
Honeydew melon	Pears
Cantaloupe	Peaches
Tomatoes	Pomegranates

Avocadoes	Kiwi
Lemons	Strawberries
Limes	Blackberries
Grapes	Blueberries
Cherries	Raspberries
Grapefruit	

Basically, enjoy any fruit or vegetable you want; just avoid bananas and carrots. Bananas are binding, and you are trying to cleanse, while carrots are really high in sugar and hard on the digestive system. Keep in mind that there are different types of tomatoes, apples, onions, and squash, so experiment with new stuff. There's green cabbage and purple cabbage, red raspberries and yellow raspberries! Yum! If possible, try to buy your vegetables from an organic market. It's definitely more expensive, but with all the pesticides being used, it's worth it. If it's a stretch financially, do a little research in your area. Many cities and towns have markets and co-ops where you can barter for lower prices by working the register a few hours a week. Also note that many markets accept EBT/Food Stamp benefits. If you still find you are unable to go organic all the way, make an effort to buy your green leafy vegetables and all your berries organic because these are sprayed the most and are affected the most due to their porous nature. Whether organic or not, always wash produce thoroughly. Use warm water and apple-cider vinegar as a natural, toxic-free produce wash.

Beans/Nuts/Legumes:

Chickpeas	Pumpkin seeds
Kidney beans	Almonds
Lentils	Cashews
Split peas	Pistachios
Black beans	Pecans
Black-eyed peas	Walnuts

While on your "Live-Food Feast," nuts, beans, and legumes will be your main protein sources. Nuts are high in protein but are also high in fat, so eat in moderation. Beans have a good amount of vitamins A and C and are low in calories. Eat them to your heart's content! FYI: beans, peas, and lentils (we're talking fresh, frozen, and dried varieties of beans and peas here) contain pentakisphosphate, which helps inhibit cancer cells from growing. Legumes and beans (red beans and garbanzo beans in particular) are also good sources of fiber, phytochemicals, and flavonols, which help fight cancer.

Condiments:

Garlic	Sprouts
Scallions	Olive Oil
Red onions	Canola Oil
Leeks	Agave Syrup*

---

*This is a sweet natural syrup that is derived from the agave plant, a cactuslike plant found mainly in Mexico. This is the same plant that is used to produce tequila. Agave is a great substitute for sugar and honey because it dissolves readily in cold beverages like iced teas and is said to metabolize itself differently from sugar in the

RECIPES

ᑎ *Guacamole*

Ingredients:

2 whole, ripe Hass avocadoes (Avocadoes should be firm but not hard. Press with your thumb. If your thumb goes in and comes out without leaving a dent, it is ready. If it leaves a dent it is overripe, and of course if your thumb does not go in, the avocado is not ripe.)

2 cloves garlic (finely chopped)

1 lime (cut in half)

2 pinches cayenne pepper

Cilantro (chopped)

1 large ripe tomato (diced)

1 pinch sea salt

Cut avocadoes in half, remove pit, and use a large spoon to scrape the avocado meat into the bowl. Cut lime in half and squeeze one half into a bowl. With a spoon, mix and mash the avocado with lime juice. Add diced tomato, garlic, cayenne pepper to taste, cilantro and sea salt. Mix thoroughly in bowl.

---

body. It does not stimulate digestive insulin secretion, as do other sugars; therefore, it is less disturbing to the glycemic index. In layman's terms: it does not create a "sugar rush." This is essential in keeping you "even" and avoiding mood swings that are often caused by sugar consumption. If you are diabetic or are at high risk of diabetes, this is the sweetener for you! Note: a little goes a long way because it is very, very sweet.

Take second half of lime and squeeze it on top of mixture. Cover bowl with plastic wrap and place in refrigerator until ready to serve.

Instead of corn chips, enjoy with celery stalks and/or cucumber slices.

❧ Berry Blast

Ingredients:
    Strawberries
    Blueberries
    Blackberries
    1 whole orange
    ½ lemon
    Crushed ice

Place the crushed ice and the berries in a blender. Cut the orange in half and squeeze both halves and lemon half into blender (use strainer to catch seeds). Blend. Pour into chilled cocktail glass and garnish with berry of choice.

❧ Simple Soup

(This soup is great if you are cleansing but just want to sip something warm and savory.)

Ingredients:
    Leeks (sliced)
    Garlic cloves (chopped)

Zucchini

Yellow squash

¼ head of cabbage (sliced into slivers)

1 cup chopped spinach

2 pinches of sea salt

1 teaspoon olive oil

1 pinch cayenne pepper (optional)

Place 2½ cups of water in medium-sized saucepan. Turn on heat—do not boil! Add garlic, cabbage, yellow squash, zucchini, and leeks, in that order. Stir slowly until cabbage looks like it is starting to wilt. Add olive oil, sea salt, cayenne pepper. Stir slowly and remove from heat. Let sit covered for five minutes. Serve in a soup bowl garnished with chopped spinach.

∾ *Yellow Split Pea Soup*

Ingredients:

2 cups water

1 cup yellow split peas (washed and drained)

2 cloves garlic

1 teaspoon curry powder

1 teaspoon cumin

1 small white onion (finely chopped)

1 tablespoon olive oil

In medium-sized pot, bring water to boil. Reduce heat and add split peas, garlic, and onions. Simmer uncovered for thirty to forty minutes, stirring occasionally until peas are soft. Add cumin, curry, and olive oil. Remove from heat and cover pot. Let stand for ten more minutes. Serve hot alone or with vegetables of your choice or small garden salad on the side.

ᘓ Divine Dressing

Ingredients:
> ½ cup olive oil
> ¼ cup lemon juice (freshly squeezed)
> 1 tablespoon apple-cider vinegar
> 1 tablespoon agave syrup
> Rosemary (finely chopped)
> Thyme (finely chopped)
> Black pepper (optional)

Pour olive oil, lemon juice, apple-cider vinegar, and agave syrup into a small bowl. Whisk for about one minute until oil becomes emulsified. Add rosemary, thyme, and pepper. Whisk again for a few seconds. Pour into glass jar and place in refrigerator until ready to serve.

ᘓ Sautee Salad

Ingredients:
> Lettuce
> Scallions
> Tomatoes
> Cucumbers

Olive oil

1 clove garlic (chopped)

½ red onion (sliced)

Vegetable of choice or a combination of asparagus, string beans, kale, zucchini, squash, mushrooms, etc.

Mix lettuce, tomatoes, cucumbers, and scallions in salad bowl. In a small pan, add olive oil, garlic, and red onion. Sautee until garlic and onions are soft and transparent. Add vegetable(s) of choice. Stir lightly until vegetables are warm and covered with the olive oil, onion, and garlic mixture. Do not fry! Remove from heat and let sit for one minute uncovered. Then spoon the sauteed vegetables out over your salad. Pour Divine Dressing over it all. Enjoy!

✎ Frozen Fruit

Ingredients:

Fruit of choice

1 tablespoon lemon juice

1 tablespoon agave syrup

Wash all fruit thoroughly beforehand with warm water. When using peaches, pears, kiwi, cantaloupe, etc. (fruit you need to slice), be sure to squirt juice of a fresh lemon onto it. The lemon will keep it from turning brown and the agave will bring out the natural sweetness of the fruit. Place in bowl and place in freezer. This is fun to do with berries and grapes. They make a great, healthy, sweet snack!

ᕤ *Fruit Spritzers*

Ingredients:

Plain seltzer water

Fruit nectar (peach, mango, papaya, etc.)

Mix ¾ cup seltzer with ¼ cup nectar of choice. Pour over frozen fruit of choice. Garnish with lemon wedge. Enjoy!

When it comes to eating healthier, be creative and have fun. Enjoy my recipes, the recipes of some of your favorite chefs, or create some of your own. Just remember that you want to cleanse your system, so be sure to avoid all the items I indicated. But for how long? Well, that, of course, depends on your Relationship Level. If you are at Level One, do the "Live-Food Feast" for three days. Level Two, do it for three weeks, Level Three, three months. You will see a difference in your demeanor, outlook, and complexion.

Celibacy

Some say that the best way to get over a man is to get under, or on top of, another one. I say the best way to get over a man is to get into yourself. But I know getting into yourself is not easy, especially when we are so used to masking our pain with outside stimulants like sex or food or clothes or drinks or, on a darker note, drugs. We are so used to reaching outside of ourselves for comfort and validation that taking time to get into ourselves can seem like an impossible challenge. Of course, it's not impossible, although you will have your challenges, cravings, and desires to face while you are working through your recovery. While you are working through your recovery, you *will* be tempted to seek solace and comfort in the arms of a man. I can pretty much guarantee it. In fact, the thought of being with someone who can distract you from what you are going through will become very appealing. You just want to feel something good, something sweet, something that can mercifully lift you out of the heaviness of the pain you are feeling. But we've already agreed that each experience in life, good or bad, is a lesson, an opportunity to grow. God is trying to tell you something, so listen.

The thing about lessons is that They Will Be Learned. Even if you choose not to get the lesson, you will be presented with situations over and over and over and over again until you get it. So get it. Deal with it. Don't drown it out with loud music, frivolous affairs, meaningless companionship, or excessive hanging out. Retreat into yourself. Lick your wounds. By yourself. The pain, loneliness, and confusion you are going through is inevitable, even necessary. By blocking the pain with distractions, you put off the inevitable. You lose the lesson. Go through it. Cry. Think. Pray. Feel your pain. Find your lesson. And *then* move on. And *then* make meeting and enjoying the company of new men a part of your agenda. Now is not the time.

Take this time to really get back into yourself before you get involved with someone else. It'll be too confusing. You can end up projecting your emotions onto the person, thinking you're in love, or make someone fall in love with you and end up hurting him. And you don't want to hurt anybody, do you? I know you don't want to hurt yourself! And you could actually hurt yourself emotionally by engaging in a casual sexual affair. You could find yourself becoming attached to this person or, worse, depending upon him for sexual satisfaction and/or companionship. Or you could end up missing your ex even more, especially if your new lover doesn't compare. You could find yourself disappointed and more despondent than ever.

I know some of you are saying you're grown and believe you can separate sex from love, and maybe you can. Good for you. That's not the point. The point is you need to rest. To pamper yourself. To purge yourself. To preserve your energy, and that means sexual energy, too. You can wisely use all the energy you are accustomed to putting into sex— getting ready for it, buying outfits, waxing in crazy places, then actually having the sex, then recovering from the sex act (vaginal soreness, infections, fatigue)—and put it into something else, like exercise or a creative project. Don't worry! You will have sex again in your life if you choose to. This is just a short period of time, a time you are choosing to set aside just for your special, sacred self. You have been through the wringer as a result of your past relationship. Sit down. Stop searching. I know your heart is hurt, but running around and sleeping around is not the answer. I know you feel lonely and wreckless, but as advised in Sarah Ban

Breathnach's book *Something More: Excavating Your Authentic Self,* "You can stand still for a moment, long enough to swear to God that you'd rather be alone for the rest of your life than endure one more minute of a destructive, unhealthy relationship with a man who does not deserve you." I think it's time to stop running away from yourself into the bed of some random, soulless man. I think it's time to take some time, according to the level of relationship, and sit with yourself. That's right: if you're coming from a Level One relationship, you have to chill for at least three days; a Level Two relationship, no sex for three weeks; a Level Three relationship, no sex for three months. You can go longer if you want or need to, but use the level system as a guide. Please remember that the time frames I am presenting to you are the minimum time frames. In fact, three days and three weeks are not even really considered celibacy but abstinence, because three days and three weeks are really not a long time at all. Neither is three months, for that matter. In the book *Sensual Celibacy,* Donna Marie Williams recommends at least six months of celibacy to truly feel the benefits of the practice. Compared to her suggestions, my time frames are just a drop in the bucket. But so be it. I don't want to overwhelm you with the idea if it is something you have never tried. But try. You might surprise yourself and find you actually enjoy holding back a bit and not sharing yourself with someone until you are really ready. You might be shocked to discover that you would rather be alone, that you would rather take care of yourself (if you know what I mean) than share yourself with someone whose devotion and worth you are not 100 percent sure of. How's that for a concept?

Masturbation

So while you are on your break, while you are consciously practicing celibacy, while you are not "doing it," what's a girl to do? Well . . . when it comes to satisfying your natural sexual urges even when you are not engaging in sex with a partner, we women do have our ways. Hey, I wasn't the first to say it, but necessity *is* the birth of invention. These days, we women are a lucky bunch because there are very many nifty inventions out there that can help you do what you need to do, which is to have an orgasm, climax, release! Yes! There are dildos in all sizes, handheld vibrators, and other mechanical stimulators. I know, I know. A dildo is not a substitute for a penis. You don't have to go out and get the biggest one you can find! A dildo is supposed to be used for stimulation—some women need penetration to reach an orgasm, and for some women clitoral stimulation is enough. Only you can figure out what will work best for you. If you are embarrassed about walking into one of those sleazy sex stores and buying your sexual paraphernalia, not to worry. You can go right on-line and order your items in the privacy of your own home, with complete discretion. Try visiting greatpleasures.com, therabbitvibrator.com, or better yet, huneypot.com, a Web site run by and designed just for us sisters. Or, if you're feeling like a little fun, throw a Huney-

pot Party. I must warn you, this one is not for the timid.
This one is for the girls who just wanna have fun!

At a Huneypot Party friends gather privately at someone's home, and a trained Huneypot hostess walks everyone
"through a unique selection of quality adult toys and sensual sundries designed to stimulate all five senses." Okay.
Get it? It's basically like a sex-toy party. The Web site says
it's open to men and women, but the one I went to was all
women, which I thought was best because I don't think I or
any of the other ladies in attendance would have felt comfortable looking at sex toys with a whole bunch of men sitting around. To be honest, though, the sex-toy part was
kind of secondary. The friend who hosted the party is a fellow photographer. She's also a jewelry maker, makeup artist,
and designer, and she has a whole bunch of really creative
friends. So at her place, in addition to the table with all the
interesting Huneypot paraphernalia, she had people there
selling earrings and blouses and dresses. It was so kool and
fun. There were healthy food options like hummus with
pita, tabouli salad, fruit, juice, water, and wine. It was wonderful and relaxed. We sat around telling funny sex stories
about men and giving each other advice about our love lives
or lack thereof. Toward the end of the evening—as a surprise from our host—a guy showed up and did a sexy
striptease, and we all laughed and giggled. Some people
even stuck money in his Speedo, but not me. I have a mouth
to feed. No spare cash to be sticking in some guy's . . . Anyway, even though initially I thought it wouldn't be my kind

of scene, I did have a good time and am glad I went. I realized that the tone of these types of parties is up to the host. If you are wild and crazy, your party will be, too. But if you are laid back and chill like my host was, that is how your party will be.

I know this may sound a bit risqué to some of you, but don't be prudish. Do whatever you can do to take care of you. Because at the end of the day, there's no need to be running around all horny and frustrated if you don't have to. Honestly, if you are keeping busy, exercising, and eating a well-balanced diet that keeps your hormones balanced, you might not be affected by bouts of horniness. I in no way wish to perpetuate the stereotype that Black women are overly sexual creatures, or that no matter what we've gotta have it. I know we have other things on our minds. I know we have other ways of channeling our energy. I know we have self-control. And I know that some days it's just best to simply "pray it away." I also know that we have menstrual cycles that throw our estrogen levels into overdrive and that at some point—either before, during, or after said cycle—a real, undeniable, uncontrollable urge to, um, merge sets in. It can be distracting. It can be all-consuming. And if you don't have a partner or are choosing to remain celibate, it can be daunting. Therefore, something must be done! And sometimes women just have to take matters into their own hands, literally. That's where masturbation comes in. I'm not going to sit here and tell you how to do it, though. I'm sure if you haven't figured it out by now, you will. Besides, no two women are alike, and few women masturbate in the exact same way. Some of you may like toys, some of you may not. Some of you may like direct clitoral stimulation, some may not. I *will* share with you the importance of making the experience fun, an event even.

Pick a time and a place—your bedroom, your bathroom, your living room, your den—where you know you can relax and you will not be disturbed. Turn off the cell phone. Run a bath for yourself. Relaxing in the tub can be a sensual experience within itself, or you may choose to stimulate yourself while relaxing in the tub. Light some scented candles. Slip into something that makes you feel sexy, comfortable, and relaxed. Masturbation does not have to be about tools or movies or fantasies. It can be all about loving yourself. Caressing yourself. So massage yourself with some scented oil. How many times have you lovingly massaged your man? When was the last time you lovingly massaged yourself? Masturbation definitely provides an excellent opportunity to get to know one's body better and to be creative. It has several benefits: stress release, self-empowerment, and a better understanding of one's sexuality. Also, when masturbating you can't get a sexually transmitted disease or a little bundle of joy, so there's a certain level of peace and relaxation that comes with masturbation that doesn't come with even the best sexual intercourse. Some women enjoy using sexual fantasy while thinking about sexual thoughts while they masturbate. If you have a creative mind, this can be interesting and liberating. You can have sex—in your mind—

with the mailman one night and the UPS guy the next! You can fool around with Will Smith on Friday or Djimon Hounsou on Saturday. That's the fun thing about your imagination—*you* create the fantasy, which is fine as long as you don't become preoccupied with sexual fantasies. Remember you are doing this to release stress, to get into yourself, to figure out what you like and what you don't like, to get used to making yourself happy—not to make yourself miserable. So you have to experiment and find out what works for you. Maybe your imagination is lacking and you like to read erotica, like all those books by Zane, while touching yourself. Maybe you like some good old reliable porn. Maybe you find it repulsive. When it comes to masturbation, it's whatever *your* pleasure is, whatever gets you to where you need to go. Just be sure to mix it up, because just like with any type of sex, monotony is a real bummer.

I have a good friend who had a favorite porno movie that she would just pop into the DVD player whenever she got her urge. She had a very stressful job as a school administrator, was a single mother, wasn't seeing anybody, and wasn't trying to have different random men coming in and out of her life and her body. So she, being the self-sufficient woman that she is, took it upon herself to pleasure herself. She'd sit in her favorite chair, pour herself a glass of wine, and pop in her movie. It worked for her for a while, until she called me one early Saturday morning, giggling. "What's so funny?" I asked. "Girl, I think I need a new porno," she whispered into the phone. "Why?" I wanted to know.

"What's wrong with the one you have, the one with the cute guy you're so crazy about?" "Well," she confessed, "I think I'm getting bored with it because I must have dozed off in the middle of everything last night. I woke up with one hand in my pants and the other on the remote control. And the movie was still playing. It's a good thing I locked my bedroom door or I would be answering a whole lot of questions from my kids right now!"

If you are a woman who has never considered masturbation, who scoffs at the idea, don't be so hasty. Chances are you've done it and not even known what was happening. We know that men have "wet dreams" and wake up with erections. The only reason we know is because what happens with them happens externally. With us it's more internal. Have you ever had a dream that you were having intercourse with someone—a real unconscious dream that you did not plan—only to wake up to find your thighs sore? You were probably masturbating in your sleep. Do you remember the first time as a little girl that you were aware of a "throbbing" down there and realized it felt kinda good? Have you ever seen a little baby girl asleep moving her hips? She doesn't know what she's doing; she just knows it feels good. But by the time she grows up, she will have had people tell her that what she has been doing is "bad" or "nasty," so she will stop pleasing herself and put the fate of her own pleasure into the hands of men who are not always competent at the task. So when it comes to masturbation, I say we revert back into the little girl who innately knows what feels good to her, knows that it is her divine birthright to feel good, and has no guilt or shame in pleasuring herself and loving every inch of her own beautiful brown body.

Physical Exam

Take time to assess your health and make sure everything is in working order. Make an appointment to see the gynecologist, podiatrist, dentist, dermatologist, and/or ophthalmologist . . . and keep it!!! Get new glasses; fix that hammertoe; have a mammogram, a Pap smear, and an HIV test. Don't be afraid to assess the damage you have done through months or years of self-neglect. When it comes to your health and well-being, ignorance is not bliss—it's beneath you. You have no excuse now anyway—you're not running around making your man dinner, worrying about his problems, helping him with his issues. Use this time on your hands to check your own engine. Know what's going on with your body so that you can make the necessary adjustments and changes in your habits and lifestyle.

New Look

Okay. Calm down. I'm not suggesting doing anything drastic like plastic surgery or liposuction or breast implants, but, hey, you're grown. It's your body, and you can do whatever you want to do with it. But all of that is so drastic and even dangerous. No. I'm suggesting small, subtle changes to your overall look and presentation that will make you feel fresh. Like a new woman. Like a better version of yourself.

You could get a new haircut. Or try braids. Or highlights. Just do something so that when you look in the mirror you are reminded that you are in a new phase of your life, that you have turned the page. If you can afford a shopping spree, go for it. Pockets a little light? Scrape up some change for something inexpensive like a new hat or scarf or earrings or sunglasses or slippers or nightgown or cute T-shirt. There has to be a shoe sale going on somewhere!!! Find it and treat yourself. Don't overdo it, but I think after all you've been through, you're due for something new. And for you edgy ladies, how about getting an extra hole in your ear or (another!) tattoo? I read somewhere that Vivica Fox got a tattoo that said "Strength Courage and Wisdom" after listening to the India.Arie song during her much publicized breakup with rapper 50 Cent. It doesn't have to be that permanent. It could be something as simple as a new lipstick shade as long as it makes you feel good about yourself, makes you look beautiful, and reminds you that you are beautiful and special.

Spirit

Prayer

Simply get on your hands and knees. Every day. In the morning and at night. Ask for strength, guidance, and wisdom during this time and know that your prayers will be answered. After asking for something, practice what I call the Gratitude Prayer. While in prayer, just list all the things you are grateful for, from the roof over your head to the food in your refrigerator to the lemon in your tea. This will help you put things in perspective. Give thanks for your pain— in it lies a lesson. Give thanks for all you have—your family, friends, and life. We all have times when things can be better, but we all know that things could be much, much worse. So be thankful, grateful, and humble as you enter into your prayers. It is here you will find the comfort, strength, and peace of mind that you are so desperately in need of during this crucial time.

Meditation

If prayer is talking with God, meditation is listening to God. Find a quiet space in your home and just sit comfortably. Maybe you might want to put on some soothing music or nature sounds to relax you and keep your thoughts calm. Because while meditating many interesting thoughts will cross your mind: some will be funny, some will be spiritual, some will be sad. Nevertheless, the key is to just watch these thoughts without judgment: see them but don't react to them. In the book *Choosing Truth*, Harriette Cole shares her insight on the practice, stating: "Meditation is not a practice that follows a specific course leading to the same end for everyone. Rather, each person's experience of turning inside is unique." So when it comes to meditation, experiment with different methods while keeping your ultimate goal in mind: to be in the moment, to be calm, to listen to what your inner voice, the voice of the creator, is trying to tell you.

Some people may prefer to do a chant such as "om," which is the universal sound for "I Am" and can serve as a calming reminder of all the things you are—strong, beautiful, unconditionally loved by the divine. Chanting is an ancient and universal practice of saying a verse or "mantra" over and over again until you reach a place of peace. It is practiced widely in India and in Buddhism—remember Tina Turner (aka Angela Bassett) chanting "Nam Yoho Renge Kyo" in *What's Love Got to Do with It*—and many people find it helps them to connect to their higher selves. But you may find it more comfortable to simply sit in silence. Sitting in silence is powerful because it helps you to know who you really are, at the end of the day, without all the noise and hustle and bustle of life. Silence will remind you of what you really want out of life and allow you to see what you are capable of accomplishing and learning. So, when it comes to meditation, silence really is golden!

Talk Fast

In the spirit of silence being golden, I have to recommend that you try a Talk Fast at some point during your recovery process. What is a Talk Fast, you ask? Well, where do I begin? I guess I'll begin at the beginning. When I was a little girl, my mother—who raised five children while running a successful school on the bottom floor of our home and maintaining a tumultuous marriage for sixteen years—would, out of the blue, announce to everyone in the house that she was going on a Talk Fast. And she would, well, just stop talking. We could ask questions, and she would answer via a notepad. As a little girl I must admit I didn't really get it. But now, as a grown woman, I totally do. It may seem selfish to some, but sometimes you have to be selfish in order to preserve your sanity. Looking back on my mother's life at the time, I can imagine how stressful her life was. How many times could she say to us—her brood of greedy, hard-headed children—clean up your room, stop fighting, no more ice cream? Or how many full-blown and unbelievably exhausting arguments could she have with my control freak of a father? And after having to communicate verbally all day for her business—which required that she interact with students, supervise staff, and address each parent's concerns patiently and sincerely—I *know* she had to be tired of talking. So she would just stop. She was still there for us—I mean we had dinner and baths and all that—but she just would occasionally do it in total and complete silence.

So now, when my world gets crazy—I just go on a Talk Fast. It's very liberating and empowering, you'll see. After a breakup is a great time to try a Talk Fast—especially if you were in a situation where you were doing a lot of arguing, explaining, and yelling. Whew! Just thinking about it makes me tired. Then on top of that you're talking to your friends about it at lunch, on the phone—you know how we are, ladies. I love us, but we do love to talk. We're a bunch of Chatty Cathies, and for the most part I love it! Giggling and gossiping makes being a woman fun! But sometimes it can be a bit much, all the talking. All the chitchat. All the noise. So, in the spirit of preserving your precious energy, you will—at some point during your self-appointed recovery time—do a Talk Fast. You have to do it for an entire day—twenty-four hours. That is the minimum requirement. Most women I know who do it end up doing it longer because it feels oh so good. Choose a day or a block of days, notify your family, stash some pens and pads around the house, and proceed to shut up.

A Talk Fast is easier for us to do in today's technologically advanced world than it was for my mother back in the seventies. Now, in the new millennium, we can always communicate via e-mails and text messages. Take advantage of all this technology at your disposal to help make your Talk Fast a success. Also take advantage of information from others who have experienced the beauty and power of silence. Especially in a time of healing, when you may be feeling many emotions. Why keep talking on the phone, reiterating it? Why call your ex—there's nothing else to say. According to Eugene Kennedy, an American philosopher: "There are times when silence is the most sacred of responses." Feeling lost? A little lonely? Sit with yourself and enjoy your silence. It's a needed and valuable part of the human—the female—experience. May Sarton, a poet, novelist, and essayist once said: "In solitude one can achieve a good relationship with oneself." She, like you and me, is not the first woman to discover the power that lies in simply being silent sometimes. Erica Jong shares: "The most important education you get is your own—the one you learn in solitude." Mary Kay Blakely told her readers, "If a woman is to know herself, then periods of solitude should be courted, planned, even embraced." But perhaps it was poet Gwendolyn Brooks who said it best: "I love being by myself. As I grow older, I love myself more than anything else. There are so many things to think about and work out." Now that's what I'm talking about. And Proverbs 17:28 states: "Even a fool who keeps silent is considered wise. . . ." So, as Deepak Chopra affirms, know that "silence is the great teacher, and to learn its lessons you must pay attention to it. There is no substitute for the creative inspiration, knowledge, and stability that comes from knowing how to contact your inner core of inner silence."

Housecleaning

Just as we are cleansing our bodies, we should also cleanse our homes, reclaim our space as our own. I know you shared intimate times and good and bad memories with your ex in your space, but now it is just you. Now you are healing you. You need to be able to do it in a space that is clean, organized, and clutter free. So take a day and dedicate it to cleaning your home. Remove anything of his—throw it out, give it away, mail it to him. Underwear. Socks. T-shirts. Out. Out. Out. Just get it out of your space. You need peace of mind. You need to live in the now. All the pictures of him or him and you together; you don't have to throw them away, but please put them away. The flowers from last Valentine's Day that are dried out but you still haven't thrown away? It's time for those to go. It's also time to put your new, clean white cotton sheets on your bed. Then, sweep your home and mop your floors. After your home is clean, light some

white candles and bless your space with a prayer of gratitude. Express thanks for your space, whether it is a big
mansion or a tiny room, acknowledging that it's yours to use
to heal, grow, and let go.

Music Matters

When I was a younger woman in my preteens, the age
when I was just getting into music and was using my al-
lowance to buy records, I found myself wondering why
most songs are about love. *Dang,* I remember thinking to
myself, *doesn't anybody ever write about anything else?* Inno-
cent and naive, I couldn't understand the fascination with
the subject. Now, of course, as a woman who has known all
too well the thrills and the thorns of love, I realize why the
subject is so often written about, sung about: everybody is
trying to figure the thing out. There's nothing like love to
make people ask themselves the hard questions. The beauty
of love has inspired many to write about it, as has the pain of
it all. And as a result, every time you turn on the radio
there's a love song blaring out of it. It could be on an R&B,
reggae, rock 'n' roll, or pop station, but inevitably the subject of love and relationships will come up. And that is why
I say this: during the initial stages of your recovery, when it
comes to those R&B station slow-jam blocks of music, you
should be afraid. You should be very afraid. Especially in
the beginning, when you're just coming to grips with your
disappointment. Listening to an hour of nonstop Luther
Vandross, Teddy Pendergrass, with a little Barry White
thrown in, topped off with that darn Sade can be heart

wrenching and kind of counterproductive at this point. The tears are already fierce. You try to keep your mind off of him, but you still think about it at work, on the train, in the car, at the store. So why should you voluntarily subject yourself to such heartache? You shouldn't. Believe me, you cannot shelter yourself from music and the subject of love from other forms of media and even simply life (there's always a lovey-dovey couple right in front of you while you wait on line at the movies, the movie you decided to go see, alone, to take your mind off of your blues). But you don't have to willingly put yourself through the unnecessary pain of the quiet storm. Don't do it. You're not ready yet. Maybe in week three of your recovery process you can deal, but right now, your wounds are too deep. You need time to feel what you are feeling. I recommend jazz, something instrumental that will give your home space the warmth of sound while giving your mind space the freedom of wordless melodies. Or better yet, upbeat music that gets you going, makes you want to move.

One weekend, exactly two Fridays after I discovered the guy I was dating was cheating on me, I turned on the radio to do some straightening up in my living room. It was the end of the week and I was in a mellow mood. Under normal circumstances I would have put on a smooth station and enjoyed some love songs while I prepared to relax for the evening. But this night, I knew better. I knew that I'd been crying, unprovoked and unpredictably, all week. I knew I was still very hurt and confused about my discovery. I knew I wasn't feeling very optimistic about love. I knew that for

the past week it had taken everything in me to get up and
take my clueless daughter to school, and actually smile and
listen attentively as she chattered on about language arts
tests and the latest lip-gloss flavor, since all I really wanted
to do was stay in the bed and cry. Of course I knew there was
no point in indulging in the wonderfulness that is the R&B
slow jam. So I halfheartedly scanned the radio stations and
discovered that since it was Memorial Day weekend, a local
station was playing the top one hundred NYC dance
songs!!!! Ladies, I scurried and danced around my living
room while listening to "Into the Groove," by Madonna;
"Come to Me," by Fonda Rae; "Ring My Bell," by Anita
Ward; "Got to Be Real," by Cheryl Lynne (belting out "It's
got to be real" felt so good); and of course the all-appropri-
ate anthem "I Will Survive," by Gloria Gaynor. And although most of those songs have the thing called love as
their theme, the upbeat dance tempo let me think and feel
without falling apart.

If you think you can do it, by all means go right ahead.
You might need and benefit from a night of crying and listening to old love songs. In fact, I highly recommend it. Just
proceed with caution. And whatever you do, or whatever
CD you decide to play, by all means leave Teena Marie
alone!!!! Nobody's that strong. And before you know it, one
day Toni Braxton's "Let It Flow" will come on at the right
time and you'll listen to it and know you're going to be okay.
And soon after, the sound of Sade's voice will no longer
bring you to your knees. Instead, you will appreciate her
heartfelt sincerity and wise insight. Then, when you're

really strong, you will get up and fearlessly put on Cassandra Wilson's "You Don't Know What Love Is." And even if you do cry, you won't die. And do you know why? Because you have claimed your experiences, the beauty and ugliness of them, and they are yours. You know why. Why he couldn't give you what you needed. Why you did what you did. Why you ignored the signs. Why you wanted him in the first place. And whatever the reasons, they are yours. Embracing them like the valued possessions that they are, you can take your experiences straight to the radio, turn to the quiet storm, feel what you feel, and get up the next morning and continue to live your wonderful, creative, music-filled life.

For now, find whomever you love to listen to—pull out the Joni Mitchell, Chaka Khan, Erykah Badu, Stevie Nicks, Sheryl Crow, Jill Scott, Aretha, Patti, Mariah: they've been through it too—and blast 'em while you clean your house. Rearrange furniture. Clean out closets. Cook your favorite meal for you! Then, make a *He's Gone . . . You're Back!* playlist on your iPod or MP3 player. Choose songs that are uplifting, strengthening, inspirational, and fun. Find songs that lift your mood, address your anger, and empower you to get yourself together.

Go for it all; mix it up. The rock, the R&B, the jazz, the salsa, the reggae!!! If it makes you feel good and helps you at this time, then add it. Google it. Download it. Burn it or borrow it. Just put it on your playlist and enjoy. I have a few favorites of my own. Following are some suggestions. You will inevitably be familiar with many of these songs and many of the artists. Some may be new to you, but check them out anyway. Regardless of the artists or genre, the common denominator in the songs that I have chosen for this list is that they are uplifting and empowering songs that I hope every woman will enjoy. The songs will make you move, they may make you smile, and they might even make you cry—but most importantly, they will serve as support for your wounded spirit. You know that pain purifies the soul, so turn up your radio or your iPod or your car stereo or whatever and do your dandiest to dance your heartache away, okay?

HE'S GONE . . . YOU'RE BACK PLAYLIST

"Bag Lady," by Erykah Badu

"Thank You," by Alanis Morissette

"Jagged Little Pill," by Alanis Morissette

"Ought to Know," by Alanis Morissette

"Would I Lie to You?" by Annie Lenox

"I Hate You So Much Right Now," by Kelis

"Shake You Off," by Mariah Carey

"Fly Like a Bird," by Mariah Carey

"One Is the Magic Number," by Jill Scott

"I Keep/Still Here," by Jill Scott

"Golden," by Jill Scott

"Slowly, Surely," by Jill Scott

"Beautiful Day," by U2

"Stuck in a Moment," by U2

"My Joy," by Leela James

"Enough Cryin'," by Mary J. Blige

"No More Drama," by Mary J. Blige

"Little Things," by India.Arie

"Gonna Get Over You," by France Joli

"I Will Survive," by Gloria Gaynor

"Three Little Birds," by Bob Marley

"Put Your Records On," by Corinne Bailey Rae

"Survivor," by Destiny's Child

"So Good," by Destiny's Child

"Me Myself and I," by Destiny's Child

"Through with Love," by Destiny's Child

"A Rose Is Still a Rose," by Aretha Franklin

"Imagine Me," by Kirk Franklin

"Bye, By, Bye," by 'N Sync

"I'm Still Standing," by Elton John

"Finally Made Me Happy," by Macy Gray

"Me," by Tamia

"The Best of Me," by Chrisette Michele

"Be OK," by Chrisette Michele

"I Will Not Be Broken," by Bonnie Raitt

"Shackles," by Mary Mary

"Can't Give Up Now," by Mary Mary

"I Need You Now," by Smokie Norful

"Alright," by Ledisi

"Fall," by Cree Summer

"Move On," by Joi

"Let It Flow," by Toni Braxton

"Keep on Movin'," by Soul II Soul

"Goodbye to You," by Patti Smythe

"Let It Go," by Keisha Cole

NEWSFLASH: Make the most of these tools and all the resources you may have at your disposal to help you stay positive, focused, and dedicated to your recovery. These things are all useful, even mandatory. It's a fight, but it can be fun. When was the last time you allowed yourself to really focus on yourself? To enjoy your music, read your books, say your prayers, listen to and hear your own thoughts, and be mindful of your actions? So take the time. Do what you need to do for you. You can do it, especially if you do it to the beat of some good music. You won't be the first and you won't be the last woman to have to pull herself up, reinvent herself, and remarkably recover from a relationship gone wrong.

Chapter 7

BOUNCING BACK

"Our greatest glory is not in never falling, but in rising every time we fall." Confucius

Life is full of bulldozers: things, events, happenings, crises, and unforeseen circumstances that leave one feeling dazed, devastated, and/or discombobulated. A death in the family, being laid off from a job, being betrayed by a friend/family member, being robbed, mugged, raped, or violated in any way are all examples of bulldozers. After one of these you feel like you've been hit *and* run over by a Mack truck. After a bulldozer you have to use all of your resources—spiritual, mental, physical, emotional, financial—to get on with your life, to start all over again, to bounce back.

The end of a relationship is one of life's many bulldozers. Especially when you didn't even see it coming. An exercise of your true strength comes from the ability to bounce back from any bulldozer. But like a bouncing ball, bouncing back from a bulldozer is often a series of ups and downs. The good days and the bad days. The feelings of optimism and hopelessness. The laughter and the pain. The moments

215

when you feel you can conquer the world and the times when you don't even want to face it. After going dutifully through your recovery—reflecting upon your relationship, doing your journaling, embracing a healthier lifestyle, practicing celibacy, enjoying your Talk Fast—you'll have newfound optimism and a whole lot of energy that can and should be used to propel you into the next chapter of your life. To bounce back, though, you will need creativity, compassion, and ultimately courage.

Giving Back

Pain propels you toward compassion. After going through loss and disappointment you can sympathize with the painful plight of others. This compassion, this understanding, no matter how hard-earned, is a beautiful thing. Now is an ideal time to cultivate it so that it can grow. Now is an ideal time to utilize your compassion to help others. You've taken time for yourself, felt sorry for yourself, examined yourself, ridiculed yourself, forgiven yourself. So it only makes sense that at some point you have to take the focus off of yourself and place it on others. When you look at it truthfully, your heartbreak over your relationship is nothing compared to the pain and suffering going on in the world around you: there is a war overseas, genocide in Africa, devastation in New Orleans, and a sad, lonely child right next door. Surely you can find someone or something worthy of a little of your time, energy, and newfound compassion. Surely you can discover a way to help someone who needs it badly.

Volunteer to hold an orphaned baby at a local hospital (after all, you know all too well how sometimes all someone really needs is a big, warm, sincere hug), become a big brother or big sister, or maybe even consider adoption or taking in a foster child (your experiences, advice, wisdom, and resources can make a real difference in a child's life). Organize a group of kids from your neighborhood and take them to the movies, the museum, or a play. If you are not into kids, do something that will help adults. Read at a senior citizens center. Set up a regular lunch date with your elderly neighbor. Go food shopping for the nice old man up the block. Contact your local library and find out how you can help adults learn to read or speak a second language. It doesn't matter what you do, as long as it is not about you. You will soon discover firsthand the wonderful benefits of exercising selflessness. Once the focus is taken off of yourself and your problems, you will see things in a new light and from a different perspective. It will become clear that whatever you've been through is not so bad after all. And all that love you have inside, the love that you held aside for him, the love that you don't know what to do with, will be appreciated and utilized by those you choose to help. And in the end you will be the better for it. You will be in awe of yourself because of your ability to give time and energy to others despite your personal pain. Your love for yourself and your compassion for others will have increased twofold, and before you know it, your mission of moving on with your life, preparing for a new mate, realizing your blessings, and practicing unconditional love will have been accomplished.

Getting Back in the Game

After all your self-reflection and selflessness you may feel you are ready to start dating again. If that's the case, let me just tell you this one thing: have fun!!! Make it a point to take it light and keep things in perspective. Although you may feel healed and recovered, you are still in a vulnerable place. But there's nothing like dating to add a little excitement and optimism to your situation. There's nothing like going out on the town with someone handsome, new, and interesting, getting to know someone via intimate conversations, and having someone laugh at your jokes or appreciate your insight. And don't forget the best part: dating is an excuse to go shopping, get dressed up, feel sexy, and look attractive. This would be a great time to step out of your routine and try new colors and styles; this would be a great time to reinvent yourself. Try a new hairstyle, pick a different color nail polish, experiment with a different shade of lipstick. You are now looking toward the future and walking away from the past, so of course you'll also need—you guessed it—some new shoes. Yippee!!! But seriously, a new look is a great idea, but when you start to date again the most important tool will be a new attitude. No one wants to be around someone bitter and angry who's griping about their ex or projecting what the old man did onto the new man. So if you find yourself pessimistic about love and relationships, if you go into the whole dating thing with an attitude that it's not going to work, expecting the worst, you probably are not ready to date just yet. You probably have more recovery work to do. You'd probably be better off renting a movie and doing your toes—staying home!—on Saturday night until you feel truly great about yourself and optimistic about your romantic future.

But if you are sure you are ready, then go for it. Get on with it already! But how? Meeting men is not always so easy, but in today's technological age, it's not impossible. I've had many friends rave about online dating, and I have even chatted with a few fellows online myself. I've never had the desire to actually go out on a date with anyone I met on-line—yet!—but I'm not against it as long as it's done with safety in mind. There are many articles and books written on the subject so I'd suggest doing a little research on different online dating services and safe online dating techniques before you start your search. Along with the information and advice you'll find while doing your research, I suggest basic common sense: make sure you've chatted online for a while before speaking on the phone. Take his number and do not give him yours until you meet and feel out his vibe. People are not always truthful so don't take everything you read about your date online at face value. If he says he's single but is acting shady and only wants to meet in dark, obscure places, consider that he may be hiding something. If he says he maxes six figures online but shows up for the date on a bike, maybe he wasn't truthful about his income or maybe he's just environmentally conscious. This is what makes meeting people you meet online in person so important. There's nothing like a face-to-face to feel someone's vibe, to know if your energies mesh. So trust your instincts. If something doesn't feel right, acknowledge it. Always meet in a public and crowded place. And don't go home alone with him or allow him into your home until you feel comfortable. It can be very tricky, but it has been effective. I personally know two couples who met online, dated a few years, and are currently happily married. And I've had the pleasure of photographing many weddings that were the result of online dating. So if you feel like taking a chance and using today's technology to your advantage, go for it. There is no longer any stigma attached to meeting people online. Just because you explore online dating, it does not mean you are desperate or crazy or lonely. On the contrary, it means you are taking matters into your own hands, putting yourself out there, finding out what your options are. So if you've always been a bit curious about online dating, give it a try. But make sure you are clear about what you're looking for. Do you want a friend, a companion, a serious relationship, marriage, children? That's the good thing about many of the best online dating services like Match.com or eHarmony.com—they force you to ask yourself questions about who you are and what you want. They force you to be clear, and you know how much I cherish clarity.

Clearly, though, online dating is not for everyone and

you may prefer to try things on your own. First, you have to go where the men are. Most cities have singles mixers and events like dating cruises or speed dating. Singles mixers are small, sophisticated parties where the only people who are invited are single. That way if you bump into a guy at one of these things you don't have to wonder if he's involved or vice versa. Sometimes friends give them in their homes but there are organizations and networks that do them, too. Dating cruises can be expensive but interesting because you get to go on a short cruise for a few days—usually something like from Miami to Bermuda— and the ship has all these fun activities aimed at singles and designed to bring people together. As for speed dating, well, the one I went to was held at an upscale restaurant in Manhattan. There were a lot of people talking, eating, drinking, and mingling but the speed-dating part was optional. I think it was like fifteen dollars to participate.

Once one signs up, they escort you into another group with the rest of the participants. Then you take a number and fill out a form with your information. Your information corresponds to the number you are given. Anyway, you, the ladies, sit down and then a guy sits in front of you. You have about five minutes to "get to know each other," ask each other questions and whatnot. Then they ring a bell or change the record or flip the light or something to signify the five minutes is up and the guy moves to the next table and is replaced by—duh—another guy. This goes on for about an hour until all the guys have met all the girls. Then at the end you give the facilitator the number of the guy (or guys) whom you are interested in, and the guys do the same. If there are numbers that match, then they give you each other's information. The one time I went I didn't give a number because—and I really wasn't being picky—no one really, truly moved me. But when the facilitator told me two guys had picked my number, I wondered if I had picked a number would it have matched. But I'll never know. I did have a good time, and I would do it again, but maybe with a crowd that is not so conservative. Anyway, what I'm saying is that there are a lot of new ways to meet people these days. I suggested these because they are, if anything, fun. Because that's really what dating should be. It should be fun, not a chore. And even if you don't meet the man of your dreams or make a connection that leads to a mate or even a future date, chances are you'll have a good time, meet interesting people, and do a little networking.

You can also put the word out to family members and friends that you are ready to start dating. Again, it may not lead to anything significant, but I'm sure you'll get a kick out of discovering whom your friends and family think you might be compatible with. I'm sure, as long as you are smart and safe, it will be fun and funny! Every girl needs a giggle!

If you don't feel comfortable with putting yourself out there like that or if you are reluctant to tackle the whole technologically advanced online dating thing, you can do things the old-fashioned way and leave it all to fate. Yup. You read me right. If you go about your business and your life doing what makes you happy, pursuing your goals and interests, putting your best face forward, and taking care of your physical, spiritual, and emotional health, you are bound to bump into someone who finds you attractive and interesting and vice versa. This approach has been very effective for me, personally. I've discovered that men find women more attractive and intriguing when they are happily pursuing their own interests and passions. So, as they say in Brooklyn, "Do you, boo." In my excursions as a writer, photographer, philanthropist, avid reader, and art lover, I've often met many smart, successful, and interesting men at museum openings, photo exhibits, cocktail receptions, book signings, film festivals, and entrepreneurial seminars. Since I was doing what I loved to do, wanted to do, and needed to do, I ended up meeting interesting and attractive men with whom I had much in common. Even though these interactions haven't led to a love connection (as of yet!), I always ended up feeling and knowing that I too was interesting and attractive. And I've made a few really good friends and business connections along the way.

If you are not interested in taking the passive role, be aggressive. Throw your own party! A *He's Gone . . . You're Back* Cocktail Party. Announce—loudly and boldly—to the world that you have survived your breakup, you are past the past and ready for the future. But that is just one objective of the *He's Gone . . . You're Back* Cocktail Party. The other objective is to meet new guys and help your other single friends do the same thing. As Black women, I know we are not used to referring other women to potential partners for many reasons but mainly because we are afraid of being blamed for a bad situation. I know I would hate it if someone went out with a guy I hooked her up with then came back to me all crying and upset 'cause he played her or broke her heart or lied to her or slept with her neighbor. So what I'm suggesting is not setting people up. I'm simply suggesting that you provide a space where people you know and like—male and female, coworkers and cousins—can get to know each other in a relaxed, intimate setting with great finger foods and creative cocktails. Before the party, make it clear to all invited individuals that, while you will do your best to invite people you know relatively well and trust for the most part, it is not your personal responsibility whom they choose to hook up with and how. Then go ahead and do it—host your party, invite some single girlfriends and eligible bachelors. Now's the time to put them in the same room, shake with a little music, add a little atmosphere, and see what happens. It's simple: every woman you invite must invite a single, straight man they know and like but are not interested in dating. We all know a few good men we would never date but would be perfect for someone else. You can opt to host it at your own home or choose another location like a nice, cozy restaurant or bar. Just make sure the lighting is good and the music is not too loud so people can talk with ease. So give it a try. You might help facilitate a great relationship or friendship between two great people. Try it again; you might meet someone you like. Try it once more; you might meet someone you love. How's that for fun!

Whatever approaches you take to the whole dating game, try to tread lightly in the ocean of men and potential mates out there. Remember that you have the power to say yes or no; always be careful, safe, and smart; and, of course, be sure to enjoy every single minute of it!!

Dating Differently

Here's a thought: how about when it comes to dating you try to do things differently? Don't panic. I'm not suggesting that you start dating women or anything, but now that I think about it, if you were ever curious, I guess now is as good a time as any. I don't have much insight to offer you on that subject, because, as for me, I'm strictly, well, you know. What I am suggesting is that you shift things a bit, step outside of your box, try something new, dare to be different. Start with looking at your patterns. Is there a certain type of man whom you have become accustomed to dating? How about flipping the script? For instance, if you are used to dating the bad boy, date a nerd! If you are used to dating older gentlemen, date a younger dude! Just try something a little different. I usually go for the boisterous, aggressive type who loves attention and needs to be seen but have found that the quiet, laid-back types are sweet and secure. Do you like the stocky, muscular, athletic type? Then go out with a tall, wiry man. It won't kill you. It will make things a little more interesting. You don't have to marry the man, and you definitely don't have to sleep with him. But one night out with someone who is sooo not your type is an interesting way to see what you are or are not missing. Because people are people, and even though we have our preferences and are attracted to a certain physical and intellectual type of man, men are men. I think sometimes we miss out on making connections with nice guys just because they don't look like what we are looking for when, indeed, personality wise, they just might be.

And of course I can't talk about dating differently without asking if you have ever or if you would ever consider dating outside of your race. Putting preconceived notions about people based on their race aside, take it into consideration. Use it as an opportunity to discover what you do like and what you do not like. Try something new! You, after all, are a new person. You are in a whole new phase of your life. Don't limit yourself to the familiar or comfortable. By opening your mind up to the idea of dating outside of your race, whole other groups to consider open up: Jewish men, Greek men, Italian men, Spanish men. Use this as a chance to, if anything, learn about different cultures, food, lifestyles, and traditions. It will make you a more well-rounded woman. So give it a try, but of course do what you are comfortable with. Just push the envelope a little bit.

Don't just push the envelope by changing the type of men you date: change the way you date. Are you naturally aggressive? Well, fall back a bit. Reticent? Try saying what you mean. If you usually let the guy take you out, take him out. Pick the restaurant. Try new activities. Never been skiing? What are you waiting for? Always wanted to visit a wine vineyard for a day? There's no day like today!

The New Crush

Let's admit it, ladies: crushes are fun! And when we are having fun, we are lighthearted and laughing. Having a crush may seem silly and immature because we are not in high school anymore! But you know what? So what! That's the whole point. Remember how much fun you had in high school when you had a crush on a guy? Remember getting the bathroom pass from science class so you could peek in on him during his gym class, in his gym shorts? Remember hanging out at the pizza place where he would always go with his friends just so you could grin and say, "Hi!" all shy-like? It was great! It was invigorating! It was exciting! Allow yourself to tap into that youthful, girlish energy. You may be a big girl now, but that impractical high schooler is still inside you somewhere waiting to come out. There's no better way to pull her out than to have a crush.

The best thing about a crush is that you can have a crush on anybody—it doesn't matter—and you don't have to even take it seriously. A crush can be someone you admire from afar, someone totally unattainable like a rock star or a public figure. Someone around whom you can create fantastic fantasies. I know a few sisters who have been crushing on Barack Obama for a good minute, and I'm not mad at any of them. Me? Well, I'm always kinda crushing on Brad Pitt *and* Djimon Hounsou—talk about different sides of the spectrum! I also know a woman in her fifties who has a crush on the nineteen-year-old security guard in her building! Whatever floats your boat.

Another good thing about a crush is that you don't have to act on it, especially if your crush is your boss or co-worker or professor (or a nineteen-year-old security guard!). Just have little daytime fantasies. Smile more. Flirt. Give yourself a reason to put on lip gloss all day or wear your favorite flower skirt sometimes. Take it light. A crush is a good thing. At least you're not obsessing about your ex anymore! At least you are not being all melancholy. No. You're laughing and playing and flirting! You're crushing and you're having fun!

Let's Talk about Sex, Baby!

Sex is good. Sex is wonderful. And sometimes sex is a necessity. There's no greater stress reliever. There's no better release. After being single for a while, celibate for a minute, handling your own "business" all the time, the desire to be with a man, to be physically intimate with a man, is inevitable. We are, after all, sexual beings. As women, our hormones rage and ebb from month to month. As women, we enjoy the penetration and passion of a man. As women, we want, like, love, and, yes, need sex. As women, if we really wanted to have sex, we could. Admit it. All you have to do is make a call, flirt a little, put it out there. There's always an old lover or new neighbor who would be more than happy to help you out. But are you ready? Are you really ready? I ask this because it needs to be asked. It needs to be considered. If you meet someone, have been dating him for a while, and feel you are ready to become intimate, well, that's a no-brainer. Or is it? Is that enough? What are your spiritual beliefs? Do you feel you need to be married or at least in a solid, committed relationship before you take the plunge into bed? If so, well, there is your answer. If you are not in any of the aforementioned situations, stick to your guns. Express this to your partner and let him know you are real and sincere about your choice. Sometimes we think a guy won't go for it, and maybe he won't—but you'll never know until you put it out there. You'll never know how he will react once you say: "I'm not interested in a sexual relationship until I am married or in a committed relationship." He will either run or rise to the challenge. He will either walk away or stay. Which is a good thing, because at least you know where you stand. At least you are living by what you stand for.

I have a good friend who met and fell in love with a really special guy a few years ago. He was sweet, but most importantly he was spiritual. So when she told him she was not interested in a sexual relationship, when she showed him how she felt about him by cooking for him, listening to him, and empowering him with her compassion and wisdom, he didn't go away. He's still there. She got what she wanted—which is what it's really all about. It's about what you want. Not what a man wants. Because as we have all learned the hard way, compromising your beliefs is never worth it in the end. Granted, she took a chance on losing him but, hey, sometimes you have to take chances. And granted, I am not there alone with them in the heat of the night, so who knows if what she claims to be is really what is. I also have no idea if he is sleeping with women other than her. I don't know. I do know that this is a strong woman who believes in her convictions and is strong in her faith. I do know that she is a woman of her word. And I do know, just by seeing them together, that this is a man who really loves her and is willing to make compromises until he can give her what she really wants: marriage.

Some men will take it as a challenge and do whatever is in their power to persuade you. Beware. Make sure you are not rushed into a relationship because of your revelation. Some men may feel they are being manipulated. But if you are clear and honest and sincere when you say what you have to say, then, hey. As Janis Joplin said, "Don't compromise yourself. You're all you've got."

But what if you are okay with the occasional, well—what else can I say—lay? What if, right now, after surviving a heart-wrenching emotional and physical attachment to a man, you are ready, willing, and able to accept "casual" sex as an option? (I put the word "casual" in quotes because I don't really think there is any such thing as casual sex. I think sex has emotional and physical ramifications. I think there's nothing casual about unwanted pregnancies, sexually transmitted diseases, or emotional attachments forged in the bedroom. But, hey, that's just me.)

In that case, honesty is still key. Don't go throwing your good loving around to any and every body. You risk getting a man attached to you, which can be a problem if you are not sure it is what you want, if you have not been clear with him about your intentions. You might be surprised to know that—duh!—men have feelings too. Men get attached too. So before you go having sex with the guy you met online or the guy from your job or the guy from the health club, make sure you and he are clear about what you are getting into. When it comes to you, make sure you weigh the stakes. Make sure sex is enough. There is no sense in pretending and lying to yourself about what you really want and need, there is no sense in not living your truth—that you really want more from a man but are settling for sex—if you don't have to or want to. You may go and say all of that about things being casual and then once the casualness of the situation sets in you could find yourself disappointed, hurt, confused. Don't do it to yourself. Be clear about what you really want. And if you know you're not ready, don't go there. Don't put yourself in situations where you will be tempted. He wants to come over, bring a bottle of wine, and watch a movie? I don't think so. But if you are feeling yourself and ready to explore your sexual freedom—because, thankfully, we are women living in a time where we are free to make choices about our sexuality—go for it. Get yourself some new lingerie; you deserve it! Stock up on some latex condoms and go for broke (just hope the condom doesn't break!). Have fun, take it light, and enjoy yourself and your sexuality. If you can do it, more power to you!

As for me, I won't even lie and say I have not had a few "casual" sexual relationships way back in the day. But after all I've experienced, I'm not there. I'd rather spend my Saturday night with a good movie and a cup of tea than opening myself up—literally—to someone whom I am not feeling like that. And believe me, I have tried. Once I allowed this guy I kind of liked to come over because I wanted company and companionship, and even though I knew I wasn't emotionally ready to be intimate with a man at that time, I convinced myself that I was grown enough and horny enough to get it on. But I couldn't do it. It wasn't even a moral or spiritual decision, I hate to admit. I just physically could not do it. This man was cute and funny and fine, but once he started kissing me, once he started touching me, I cringed. My body physically recoiled. Luckily he was a gentleman, so it was no big deal, but I did put myself in a vulnerable situation. Which is why I stress—be careful. My guest could have been seriously crazy, gotten mad, and physically hurt me. But God is good and it didn't go down like that. And speaking of God, maybe it was a spiritual thing. Maybe my body couldn't go there because my heart wasn't there, because my spirit wasn't there. I don't know for sure, but I do know that when it comes to postbreakup sex, it's imperative that a woman listen to herself and be honest about what she really wants, what she is really looking for. If not, she could find herself in an unfortunate and vulnerable situation. And who has time for that? We are too busy bouncing back, getting our lives on track. So before you "take a lover," make sure everyone's cards are on the table. Then go ahead, grown woman, and play your hand. Just be sure not to gamble with anything you are not willing to lose.

Claim It!

Whether you are dating for fun or looking for true love, you have to know what you want before you can recognize it when it arrives. So on that note, try to see yourself in your ideal relationship. I know we are talking about visualization here, but don't even worry about or focus on what your ideal mate looks like. Just see what you look like, what your life looks like. Are you smiling? Are you healthy? Where are you living? Is your perfect home a metropolitan condominium or a quaint country home? Do you go to your dream job every day or are you working from your home office? Are you near the water or by the mountains? See yourself living your life the way you really want it to be. See yourself being the woman you know that you are. Once you can see it, you can create it and you can claim it, this sweet life of yours. The man is just the cherry on the pie. You are the pie, and your hopes, dreams, and aspirations are the gooey fruit filling. Isn't it delicious?

NEWSFLASH: Bouncing back is all about exercising your resilience by reclaiming your life. Reclaiming your life will mean different things for different women. The above are just a few suggestions. Whatever you do, don't be afraid to take chances; don't close yourself off to the wonderful possibilities of the world or shun opportunities at finding love just because you've had your heart broken. When bouncing back, think of yourself as a ball. Bounce around a bit. If something or someone feels right, hang out a while. If not, bounce! Right now you have no commitments or obligations (other than to yourself and/or your children). So enjoy your flexibility. Take a moment to seriously think about some activities—such as going back to school for that second degree, finishing that novel, taking up a new sport or hobby, joining a book club, taking up gardening, learning a new language, adopting a pet, moving to a new city, changing careers, losing those last ten pounds, becoming more active in your church—that will help you redefine yourself, enjoy your life, put things in perspective, and basically, beautifully, brilliantly bounce back.

Chapter 8
FINALLY FREE

"Life is short. It's up to you to make it sweet."
Sadie Delaney

So what was it all for? The relationship ended and you chose the high road instead of the low one. You chose to pamper yourself instead of beat yourself up. You made a conscious decision to heal your heart and not harbor the hurt. You are no longer crying. You are shining. You did the work. Followed your Recipes for Recovery and stuck to the plan. Yeah, you might have fallen off once or twice, but you got right back on and continued the process. You've licked your wounds, forgiven yourself for your mistakes, accepted your role in your relationship's demise, faced the fact that it is over. Yet you can't help but wonder—what was it all for? Well, I'll tell you. It was all for you, for your release, for your freedom.

After any of my breakups—regardless of how bad it was or how much I was hurt or how bad I hurt the other person—all I wanted to do was to be free. I didn't want to be mad at anybody. After all, all I ever had was the best of intentions. So why should I hate someone who chose not to be with me? Why should I hate myself for choosing not to be with someone? Stuff happens. People meet and hook up for a reason and/or a season. There's really no need to be mad about it or stuck in it. But still. Like we all know all too well, when dealing with the end of a relationship, so many things come into play: pride, ego, fear, doubt, and jealousy. It gets very confusing, and trying to figure it all out only makes you feel emotionally trapped, especially when you are continually trying to figure out a conversation or situation that happened a while ago. The only solution is to let it go, decide to be free. Free from resentment, free from anger, free from hatred, free from fear.

What *is* freedom, though? I think it's the ability to do what you want and need to do without guilt or fear. I think that it's embracing your God-given right to be open to life, living fully in the present, having faith in the future, and not being burdened by the past. But what does freedom feel like? What does it look like? For me, freedom looks like me, right now in this moment (and trust me—it took me a while to get here). I am sitting at my desk at home, I am writing, I am physically, spiritually, and emotionally healthy, doing exactly what I love with my life, and content with my choices regarding my relationships and my career.

What does freedom look like to you? How does it feel? See yourself free. *Feel* yourself free. Where are you? What are you doing? Are you at a party dancing? Are you swimming in the ocean? Are you at dinner with friends laughing your head off? Are you climbing a mountain? Are you on a hike? Are you on your knees pruning your rose garden? Are you running in a marathon? Are you teaching a salsa class? Or are you directing a film? Are you happy, glowing, and content? Are you smiling on the inside and out? Are you no longer mad at anyone, especially yourself? Decide what freedom looks like and feels like for you and then claim it and keep it and never let it go. It's a beautiful feeling, and it's yours to cherish. You own it, so hold on to it. Be thankful and grateful for it. Keep the feeling and the vision in your heart. Put it there in place of past pain and lost loves. Smile into it, knowing that it is always there, this freedom, and whenever you feel it being threatened by old memories, negative emotions, or hurtful people or situations, you can go to it at any time and any place, see it, feel it, and free yourself. Because the thing about freedom is that it is not a given. You have to fight for it. It will be, basically, like fighting for your life because without freedom you are chained to the past—past choices, past mistakes, past lovers—and will be unable to move into your future. And that is no way to live. So fight. Fight to be free from bitterness, anger, and pain. Fight to be free to live your life full of light. Fight to be free to love yourself and to love another. The feeling of freedom that you have identified and placed in your heart will be your tool in this fight for your freedom. By removing all feelings of resentment and regret and replacing them with your own feeling of freedom, you will be keeping your heart light. The importance of and phenomenon of a light heart is an ancient one. Even in Egypt, the goddess Maat is depicted holding a scale. On one side of the scale is a heart and on the other side there is a feather, yet the scale is even. Her heart is

as light as a feather! Many people, historians, Egyptolo-
gists, and Kemetians, have analyzed this in many ways and
have identified Maat as being symbolic of many things—
order, balance, beauty, etc. But from what I can interpret,
she is saying symbolically, "May your heart be as light as a
feather." And this is my wish for you. That your heart be as
light as a feather. That you learn to really release those feelings and emotions that weigh you down, that make you
hateful and heavyhearted. That when it is all over—this
challenging, beautiful, painful, fantastic, fabulous life—
you have not carried all your baggage all your life. That you
have lived life unencumbered by heartbreak and loss. That
you finally, at some point, put it down, let it go, and lived
life to the fullest. That you learned your lessons and lived to
laugh about them. That you gained the thing that only time
and wisdom can give you: peace. Beautiful, real, freeing
peace. That you went through all that you went through and
still made it to the other side with your soul and your smile
intact. That no matter what, you lived life happy, content,
pleased with yourself, proud of your decisions, at peace
with your past, and clear about your future.

Be forewarned. Freedom has a price. Not everyone you
know is going to want to see you free. You'll be surprised.
Friends, coworkers, and especially exes may find your newfound freedom unsettling. Like when someone who has
been obese all of her life and has settled into the "fat friend"
role drops a hundred pounds, people who "knew her when"
do not know how to act. It's going to be the same with you.
You might not have lost physical weight, but once you lose

that emotional weight, it will show. People will notice when your face is not all scrunched up, your mouth is not in a permanent smirk, you're not sucking your teeth or saying something sarcastic under your breath when a couple walks by, or you don't scoff while reading the wedding announcements in the *New York Times* or *Jet* magazine. They are not going to know what to do with you because—I know you know it—misery looves company. I mean loves it! Miserable people want you to be miserable right along with them, all the time. They will try to say little things that remind you of your past hurt—you simply remind them that you are not into opening old wounds. They will try to hit you with dismal statistics about your age or your race or whatever—you simply smile and know that you are living according to God's plan and that everything you have earned and deserve will come in due time, and right on time. They will try to tell you about what your ex is doing, whom he was seen with, and what kind of car he was driving in order to pull you back there, make you mad, incite your jealousy—you simply tell them that you wish him the best and are glad that he is happy. Or better yet, you don't have to tell them anything. Better yet, you can just steer clear of these people—and you know who they are, and if you don't, you will—and enjoy your newfound freedom with some new, different, more positive people. Because when you get to that good place, you can't (and shouldn't) hide it, suppress it, ignore it, or underestimate it, but, baby, believe it: when you're Finally Free you and only you will be the first to know.

You'll know you're Finally Free when:

✦ You accept that whatever is meant to be will be.

✦ You see your breakup as the blessing it truly is.

✦ You are able to face the real truth about your relationship.

✦ You are able to smile about and appreciate the good times and let go of the bad times.

✦ You wake up in the morning thankful to the creator for a new day, whether or not you have a mate.

✦ You can see clearly what you do have instead of focusing on what you do not have.

✦ You refuse to be disrespected on any level, by anyone, at any time, in any way.

✦ Your goal in life is to be a better person for you, not for anyone else.

✦ You make better life choices that exemplify your self-love.

✦ You are not desperate to be in a relationship, no matter what, or by any means necessary.

✦ You are content with yourself, and where you are in your life, right now.

✦ You are not hateful or jealous when a friend announces her engagement. You are happy because you know that if it can happen for her, it can happen for you.

✦ You really know that, yes, you *are* too blessed to be stressed!

✦ You are no longer waiting for him to call or visit, and

when he does you are polite and pleasant, not sad and sarcastic.

✦ Your dreams are of the future, not of the past.

✦ You don't cringe every time you hear his name.

✦ You live your life in the present—not making choices based on "when you get a man" or "if we were still together."

✦ You meet a man and immediately wonder if he'll make a good friend, not a good husband.

✦ You walk your path in life by faith, not by sight, because you know, despite the "odds" and "statistics," you are a good and valuable woman. You are real. You exist. And if you exist, the perfect person for you does, too.

✦ Your new man is not paying for the mistakes the old one made.

✦ You can love like you've never been hurt before.

✦ You are not afraid to get close to a man because you know no matter what, if he leaves or if he stays, you're going to be just fine.

✦ You are at peace with the past, present in the present, and focused on the future.

He's Back. Now What?

So you've moved on with your life, have let go of the past, and are living happily and actively in the present. You are content with yourself and are so busy living and creating the life you always wanted that your ex rarely crosses your mind anymore. And then, out of the blue, when you least expect it—bam!—he resurfaces. He wants to see you. He needs to talk. He calls you, stops by, sends you flowers and jewelry. He calls your friends. Shows up at your job. He does whatever he has to do to get back in touch with you because, let's face it, when a man really wants to get in touch with you, he will. It's like Dolly Parton sings: "Here you come again, just when I'm about to get myself together. . . ."

It has happened to me, it has happened to friends, it most likely has or will happen to you. It's a freaking phenomenon! It's as if the power of self-love, self-acceptance, and true contentment is so strong that it attracts exes back into your life with no effort of your own. Sometimes it's a good thing, a blessing, especially if you still have love for the man. Sometimes all two people need is time and space to see things clearly, work on themselves, and diligently deal with their own issues before they can really embrace the reality and responsibility that comes with being in a real relationship. After all, if you have been actively and successfully working on yourself, if you have been resolving your personal issues, who's to say that he has not been doing the same? Sometimes all some relationships really need is time. Sometimes love can and should be salvaged. Sometimes a breakup is the best thing that could ever happen to a relationship. Sometimes people need some space and time to know if they are really ready to make the relationship work, once and for all. Maybe your man really missed you. Maybe he is really ready. Sometimes space and time can give someone a chance to appreciate you and realize how special and unique you are. Maybe he needed time with you out of his life to know that he wants and needs you in it for real and for good.

Sometimes, though, a man's return is not about you. He may think it is, but it is not. Sometimes it's unfortunately about them and their need to be needed, wanted, desired by you.

Let's face it. Many men are ruled by pride and want to be wanted, needed, and desired. And when you are no longer there, when they can feel that you have let go, they may feel the need to pull you back in. But this is for the sake of their own ego and not necessarily because they really love you, not necessarily because they are ready, willing, and/or able to love you for real. So if/when your ex shows up out of the blue wanting to talk, wanting to see you, wanting to reconcile, ask yourself some really hard questions before you allow yourself to be enticed by the event. Ask yourself, Why now? What has changed in my life? Have I recently won the lottery, come into an inheritance, or landed a new, high-paying job? Did I get a new man? Am I happier now that he is no longer a part of my life? Could he be gold-digging, jealous, trying to sabotage my progress?

Think about it. When you were crying and begging and praying to make it work, he wasn't interested. And now all of a sudden he wants to come back? Be with you? Do all the things and be the man you always wanted him to be? Take a deep breath. Blink your eyes so you can see clearly, so you can see past your own desires and longings. Make sure he's back for the right reasons. You have to make sure it's not to quell his own jealousy or need for control. It's sad but true so don't let your own ego and newfound self-esteem—as in "that's right, I'm the sh—, he finally realizes he lost a good thing," etc., etc.—alter your judgment and make you make a decision based on your ego and pride and not on true love and compatibility.

In some cases, getting back together may be something that is not even considered. If someone has hurt you too much and disappointed you and enough is enough, reconciliation may be something that shouldn't happen. If he was abusive or controlling and you can see at first sight that he has not changed or evolved, be strong. Be smart. Be clear. No one takes rejection well, so especially be safe.

In some cases, reconciliation should be completely out of the question. If you managed to remove the drug-dealing boyfriend and his insidious element from your life it would be wise not to go back there, no matter how good he looks, no matter how sweet he is, don't you think? The same goes for any type of abuse. Why would you go back to someone who beat you, or verbally abused you, or stole from you, or cheated on you over and over and over again? Why would you put yourself in the position to be hurt all over again by the same person? Because to be hurt a second time around by the same man is truly tragic even though you know if you get hurt again you will be all right, you will bounce back, you will land on your feet. You now have all the tools you need to recover from a broken heart. Which really is one good thing about surviving a breakup—the knowing that you can and will survive. After being despondent and de-

pressed, going to a dark place, then coming through it toward the light, you know that a broken heart is not going to
kill you (even if sometimes it feels like it!). Be cautious and
extremely careful about allowing any type of unification
with a man whom you know was really Mr. Wrong, someone who beat you (with fists or words), belittled you, de-
graded you, and disrespected you. You've come so far. You
may still really love this person despite his faults, but if
there ever was a time to consider your well-being, to know
your truth, to love yourself, it would be now.

But if it was something that was situational—as in he
didn't have a good-enough job at the time, maybe he really
just wasn't ready, maybe he had to move away for work and
you both agreed not to attempt a long-distance relationship—maybe the time is right now. If you are considering
his proposition of reconciliation, date him again. Go slowly.
Go to the movies. Go out to dinner. Walk through a museum. Take your time, even if this is someone you've known
for years. Act like you've just met him. And please pace
yourself before becoming intimate with him again because
sex can, will, and usually does cloud your judgment (especially if you two were extremely sexually compatible or if
you haven't had sex in a while, chile . . .). You want to be
clear when making this decision. You don't want your head
to be clouded by passion and lust. Be aware that he's come
back into your life for one of two reasons: he misses you and
is feeling lonely but has no intention of really doing anything different, or he has really worked on himself, made
significant changes and adjustments, and is really and truly

ready, willing, and able to be the man you want and need in
your life. It's up to you to figure out which situation you are
dealing with.

If you still love him, you may find yourself considering
letting him back into your life despite what you all went
through. This is true especially when he comes back—as he
should—with flowers and a ring and a house and promises
of love, devotion, and happily ever after. It might be hard
for you to say no, especially if a reunion is something you
have been dreaming about and praying for. But don't let the
fanfare fool you. Make sure. Talk to him and, most importantly, ask him—and yourself—pertinent questions.

Be sure to set aside some time to sit alone and really remember all the things about the relationship that you didn't
like and then look at him and see if those things have
changed.

Also make a list of the good things so you can remember
those, too. But identify the problems and issues first, because it's easier to remember the good times and forget the
bad times. Whatever you do, don't forget the bad times!
Were you happy? Content? Were your needs being met?

Even if you decide to reunite, feel free to take your time.
Don't rush back into anything. Maybe you need more time.
Maybe you've gone back to school and don't have the inclination to devote energy to a relationship. Maybe you're enjoying the single life. Maybe you've recently started seeing
someone and want to see how it goes. Maybe you have recently discovered some newfound talent and interest that
you want to cultivate, embrace, or explore and you know

you are not in a mental place to commit yourself and adjust your life to a relationship. If you need some more time, don't be afraid to ask for it. If he really loves you he will trust you and accept your position. If he is unwilling and unable to give you the time you need, well, there you have it.

Ultimately whatever you decide, no matter how careful and cautious you are, know that you will be taking a chance. That's simply how it goes with matters of the heart. You just have to figure out if it's worth it to you. Make sure it's what you want. Most of all make sure you are doing it for the right reasons, not out of fear or doubt or desperation. When faced with a decision like this, many of your old ideas about yourself and your life can resurface. You may wonder if you will ever meet anyone else, if he's the one and you are letting him get away again, if this is your one and only chance to be married. To all this I say don't be ridiculous and certainly don't allow these and other antiquated ideas to creep into your head and force you to make a decision that you could regret—or relish!—for the rest of your life.

NEWSFLASH: If you find yourself faced with the decision of whether or not to reconcile with your ex, don't worry. You'll be ready. Just remember to say a silent prayer for strength. If you forget, though, I'll take this time to say one for you.

Dear Lord:
Please let this child think before gazing lovingly into
_____'s eyes. I mean, Lord, we all know he's fine. And

sexy. We also know he's been a source of pain and disap-
pointment. And she's doing so well, Lord. So let her stay
focused on you. Let her remember all the bull, uh, stuff
that he put her through. Give her the strength and in-
sight she needs to make this decision. Amen.

All right now, ladies. And good luck. Whether you choose
to embrace him or reject him, it's your call, because you are
clear. About what you do and do not want. You are focused
on your future and so past the past. And you are thankfully,
miraculously, beautifully, finally free.

AFTERWORD

by Janeula M. Burt, PhD

When I was first asked to write an afterword for *He's Gone . . . You're Back,* I immediately said yes, because it was something that I knew I had a great deal of experience with, admittedly . . . a lifetime. But just as quickly as I said yes, I was hit with another emotion with the same speed and power: "Oh my God! I can't do this. Because, after what seems like a *lifetime* of being with a series of Mr. Wrongs, who's going to listen to what I have to say? What can I tell my sisters if *I* haven't healed myself? Am I a serial Mr. Wrong dater? Have I grown from my experiences? Do I feel confident enough to consider myself to be T-H-E woman? Am *I* comfortable being a single woman?" So, I had to attack this assignment with the dual duty of figuring out whether *I* had not only learned "the right way to get over Mr. Wrong," but also whether or not I was doing all of the constructive things that I should be doing in order to grow not only stronger, but wiser from my experiences.

Ouch! Thanks a lot, Kerika!!! There's nothing like holding up the proverbial mirror to yourself and looking back over "one-plus" years (I'm not gonna say exactly how many) of experiences with the opposite sex. Reading Kerika Fields's erudite and thoughtful analysis is (and was) like pulling the Band-Aid off of the ugly scab on your knee. Just like when you pull the adhesive away from the tender skin and fine hairs around the scar, you find yourself biting your lower lip as you turn each page. I found myself flippantly turning some pages and arrogantly ready to pull off the bandage with one fell swoop . . . until I turned to another page and found that the skin and the adhesive was just *a little* too strong to tug it all off at one time.

Admittedly, I am *not* a big fan of self-help books for women. Primarily because I feel that we can't fix our relationship woes with men until *they* are equally as interested and willing to fix themselves as we are. However, I am fully supportive of self-help that is proactive and supportive of women and is centered on how *we* can love ourselves and be the best that *we* can possibly be, for ourselves, and not for anyone else. Whether you consider yourself to be Superwoman or Wonder Woman, we all have good and bad days. . . . Some of these days are related to our careers, our families, our friends, our coworkers, or our man. However, we don't find the same number of books devoted to how to get along better with our coworkers or how to have a better relationship with our mothers. Nope, we spend millions of dollars on how to attract, keep, and maintain a relationship with a man. Books that tell us how to get ourselves together so that we can be better girlfriends, fiancées, or wives . . . for them, and not for us.

Unfortunately, we read books that tell us what "rules" to follow in order to find "wedded bliss" or how to date like men, so that we can give the illusion of being "strong enough" to deal with whatever bullsh— they throw our way. We read books that tell us to go to church, home-improvement stores, and to put honest and well-thought-out profiles online. However, the push to self-enlightenment in most self-help books is with the purpose of getting rid of that *dreadful* single status of yours. Is it any wonder that a man living in his mother's basement, having several "baby mamas," being terminally (and purposely) unemployed, being a married, serial cheater, or overall being completely irresponsible for the choices that he has consciously or sub-consciously made in life feels that *he* is the winning ticket in the loser lottery? Men know that women fear being single worse than they fear death. . . .

He's Gone . . . You're Back helps women to understand how we can (and should) constructively work through *one* of the *many* relationship losses that we will suffer in our life-times. And admittedly, we put much more emphasis on our relationships with the men in our lives because of our his-torical, spiritual, social, economical, emotional, genetic, cultural, psychological, and physical connection to them. Particularly in the African-American community, we are so "ride or die" for our men (and boys) that they have probably lost the ability to be "ride or die" for us. Yes, Black men have it hard . . . but Black women have it hard, too. Particularly since we socially (and genetically) have a tendency to take on the woes of those around us (e.g., our men, our families, our friends) while sacrificing or ignoring our own personal needs.

Rather than focusing on healing ourselves so that others will want us, *He's Gone . . . You're Back* focuses on healing yourself because it is the right thing to do . . . FOR YOU! We've all reached the *point of no return*, not once . . . but multiple times, in our relationships. Yeah, I was that girl who caught her man kissing another woman on the street in front of her car. But instead of letting the relationship go, after what I had seen with my own eyes, I ran through a dangerous, unknown, dark alley, so that I could hear him tell me that the kiss meant nothing. Rather than accept that he really wasn't that into me, I wanted for him to tell me that this THIRD woman in his life (that I know of) was mean-ingless. He couldn't break up with the first one, because she was crazy and would probably try to kill herself if he left her . . . again the dread of being *single*. And I didn't want to have that kind of guilt on my head. So, I hung in there. . . . But here was this third woman, an old college "sweetheart" who had rekindled some old feelings in him. It didn't matter that we shared a love of good wine, art museums, and poetry. It didn't matter that he was as cool as a breeze with my friends, that I inspired him to pursue his dreams, or that we shared a little Soror/Frat love. In the end, it didn't matter because not only was he just being SELFISH . . . he was having his cake and eating it, too. Ultimately, no matter how much *mad love* he had for me, he had more *mad love* for bachelorette number three . . . whom he married, and I think is still married to.

It is a sage person who understands the profundity of the old adages "Everyone that is like you, is not for you" and "You can't judge a book by its cover." We all remember sitting in the back of our wood-paneled station wagon (see, I'm showing my age now) or minivan and saying, "When I grow up, that's gonna be my car!" Whether it was a Porsche, Mercedes, Mustang convertible, or Cadillac, we imagined ourselves behind the wheel of this fantastic car . . . not a worry in the world. No gas, no insurance, no wear and tear, no oil changes, no new tires, no car note . . . just a shiny, new, beautiful car. But after you buy your first car, you quickly learn that your wants, desires, and expectations for the car fall very short of the realities of owning a car, any car . . . luxury or not. You quickly learn that a car is only the means for getting you from point A to point B . . . period. If you only ride around in your car and never check the tire pressure, change the oil, wash the car, or do the scheduled maintenance . . . you are asking for trouble. And if you have to think about whether to pay your mortgage/rent or to pay your car note . . . there's a problem. Hopefully, we get to a point in our lives where we realize that a car is just a car, and we should buy a car that fits our personal needs, finances, and style. I think that a lot of women approach relationships like they are shopping for a car, with a long list of superficial wants.

When it comes to relationship levels, I think that we also have to be honest with ourselves in rating what we feel is or was our relationship level with our man. A friend and I are fans of a former soap-opera star whom we believe if she really knew us would be our BEST FRIEND. But the reality is that she doesn't really know us, so that friendship really exists in our heads. So we laughingly call her "our *best friend* . . . in our heads." Something she really got a kick out of when we did finally meet her (smile). Years ago, I came up with the question that I think is much more effective than asking a man if he is single. Most men would almost always answer that they were single when posed with the question . . . because "in their head" they weren't married, so they were single. So, I decided to go further and ask the question of whether there was a woman (or women) out there who *thought* that *they* were his girlfriend, fiancée, or wife. More often than not, they laugh and say that I'm "funny" for asking that question . . . but the responses that follow tend to be a lot more telling. More often than not, the laughter disarms the lie, and they end up saying things like, "Well, yeah . . . there is this girl, but we aren't all that." Or "Well, yeah, I'm married . . . but my wife and I aren't happy; she doesn't like sex." Okay, that was half truth/half lie. You would be surprised what you hear from men who are in "relationships" about what they think their relationship level is. Now, he may share the same relationship level (Level One, Level

Two, or Level Three) that his girlfriend (or nongirlfriend) has when he is with her, and those who know her. But I think that the real test of a relationship level is what the "standard deviation" (sorry, shop talk) is between what he says and she says when they are apart. Sometimes it is the gap (or deviation) between what he feels (or thinks) and she feels (or thinks) that can and should cause her to *Ready? Set. Let Him Go!*

I had a Latina sister friend describe her Abyss as "the couch of disempowerment." It was the couch that she sat or laid on when she was depressed about a failed relationship and ate comfort food, drank a few beers, and cried until she couldn't cry any more. Her couch was the place where she felt that all of her energy was sucked out of her until she felt powerless and unpretty. It was a part of her routine and how she was able to work through a relationship that had just ended. While it was true that a lot of energy and power were being sucked out of her emotional psyche, it is probably more accurate to describe this process as allowing the negative energy, toxins, and powerlessness to be taken away from her and into her massive couch . . . so that when she finally did rise from the couch, she was shedding all of the contaminants of her past relationship, so that she could be free to move on.

Another thing that I continue to be fortified and strengthened by is the knowledge that I am never alone in the process of getting over Mr. Wrong. I have wonderful friends (both male and female) who keep me sane and grounded. For example, my male friends, as guys will, do the awkward hug (and a pat) and with their "shake it off" demeanor slap you on the rear end and say, "Don't worry about it; he was a clown anyway." End of story. But the one friend who comes to mind is my good friend Donna, whom I met while I was in graduate school in the Deep South. A true *steel magnolia* to the core, who stopped speaking to her grandmother until she apologized for calling me the N-word in a conversation. It was during the initial stages of my friendship with Donna that I realized that white girls don't have it any easier than Black girls do when it comes to relationships. Even in a place where being engaged (with a big rock) before you declare your major was not that unusual. I watched with wide-eyed amazement as she and her friends dated in the world that we Black folks had developed mythical folklores about. But the reality is that their world was not much different from ours. The biggest difference I found was that even though they played the field as much (or more) than brothers did, Southern white men knew that their goal was to eventually find a wife and start a family.

Sometimes it takes someone who is not a part of your culture or experience to help you see clarity about you and your experience. For example, it was I who showed Donna having a college degree did not equal being a great man. Thankfully she listened to me and is now married to a sage, patient, hardworking, and loving man . . . without a degree. And it was she and I who came up with the concept that whomever we ended up dating and eventually marrying would have to be what we considered to be the "Future Mr. Burt/Mr. Davis." Not only would he have to love us unconditionally, he would also be expected to love and respect our friendship as well. And again, her husband, Scott, fit the bill . . . and he is as much a part of my support system as she is. For example, if I need a pity party, he's right there at the Winn-Dixie buying steak, potatoes, and ice cream. But one of the most enjoyable aspects of our relationship is that when I am trying to get over Mr. Wrong, all I have to do is call Donna (or Scott) and say, in my pitiful voice, "I need to hear the 'fabulous Jan' speech." Instinctively, she starts going off and listing all of my positive attributes, accomplishments, and things that she most admires about me. And by the end of her tirade, she usually ends with "and if whoever the jacka— is who doesn't know to appreciate these things about you, F him!" Followed by, "So what happened?" Somehow, it's a lot easier to tell my *truth* after I have heard how fabulous I really am, because I feel less like a victim and more like someone who is ready to move on.

In speaking about how *your truth can set you free*, Donna was quick to remind me how I came to her rescue while we were in school and she was so delusional and "in love" with her Mr. Wrong. She took care of his every need, which included buying a wedding dress in anticipation of his proposal and giving him money to keep his truck out of repossession. But when she drove long distance to "surprise" him, it was she who was truly surprised by him with another woman. So we did what most girls would do: we got drunk and talked junk about him. Long story short, as she told me about him and their relationship, and what she *should* have done, I stopped her dead in her tracks when in my inebriated state I said, "Why are you stressing about him? He has bad credit. . . . You are far too fabulous for that!" She couldn't help but laugh as we continued to list all of the bad points that she never would have admitted to anyone while they were in their relationship—punctuating each fact with . . . *AND* HE HAS BAD CREDIT! Needless to say, her Mr. Wrong was a little easier to get over, with those five little words. Rather than ending the evening in tears and continual pity, we ended it in laughter. Donna's *truth*, as silly as it was, not only released her from her relationship with Mr. Wrong, but also made her realize that the love that her Mr. Wrong had for her was a phony love, while hers was much more powerful and truthful. It is impossible for a "phony" and a "powerful" love to occupy the same space, because eventually the "powerful" love will either suffocate or overpower the "phony" love—they cannot occupy the same space equally.

It is important to not only note but also to acknowledge and to mourn the loss and the impact that the relationship had in our lives. So before we move on, we have to make sure that we not only recognize that the loss occurred but to figure out what we can learn from this experience. And once we are able to figure that out, as women, we need to find the best path to *constructively* nurture and heal ourselves. And depending on the relationship, the *recipe for recovery* may be different each time you find yourself recovering from Mr. Wrong. Whether it's having a good cry, reading trashy novels, taking an African dance class, hosting a pity party, running a marathon, taking several aromatherapy baths, singing in your church choir, volunteering at a women's shelter, or simply looking and feeling fabulous despite him, it is important that you find the perfect combination that brings you back to being the most fabulous woman that you can possibly be. No one can tell you exactly when you will *bounce back* from your recovery, but the more focus that you put into not only learning from your experience but also healing from it, the easier it will be to go back to being your regular, loving, happy, fulfilled self, FREE to love *yourself* first and others later.

Like any reader, I wanted to finish *He's Gone . . . You're Back* so that I could hear that now that I'd read this vital and essential book, my life and my story were going to have the proverbial happily ever after ending. That now that I'd traveled down the yellow brick road . . . my prince would be waiting there with a slipper that was meant for me and me alone. And yes, I know that I am mixing my fairy tales. However, after turning page after page, happily at times, and tentatively at others, I got to the end and found that there was no kiss that was going to wake me from this restless slumber and end this perpetual sea of Mr. Wrongs. And, unfortunately, I found myself left staring at the scar that I had so cautiously and carefully been removing throughout my journey through this book. But then I was struck by something Kerika Fields's grandmother Marie had said: that scar was "something that I could share on my deathbed." But who has time to wait for death to come stealing to share the interesting, tragic, ironic, and funny (much after the fact) stories that lie behind the scars on my knees, elbows, shins, buttocks, and, yes . . . my heart. Like one of my favorite S-heroes, Zora Neale Hurston (1928), after reading *He's Gone . . . You're Back,* I feel even more empowered and powerful because I know that: "I am not tragically colored. . . . I do not belong to the sobbing school of Negrohood who hold that nature somehow has given them a lowdown dirty deal and whose feelings are all hurt about it. No, I do not weep at the world—I am too busy sharpening my oyster knife."

Janeula M. Burt, PhD, is an educational psychologist, a research consultant, an adjunct professor, and a freelance writer. Originally from East Hartford, Connecticut, Dr. Burt earned her Bachelor of Arts degree in Political Science from Howard University in Washington, D.C., and a Master of Education in Higher Education Administration and a PhD in Educational Psychology, both from Auburn University in Auburn, Alabama. Her research experience is in the areas of African-American education, school reform and accountability, technology in education, education program implementation and evaluation, early childhood education, teacher education, student development, rural education, and African-American identity development. As a published writer, her works have appeared in anthologies such as *Souls of My Sisters* (2000), *Gumbo for the Soul* (2007), and *Souls of My Sisters Revisited* (2008). Although originally initiated at Howard University, she is an active member of the Washington, D.C. Alumnae Chapter of Delta Sigma Theta Sorority, Inc. Dr. Burt served as the Chair of the Arts and Letters Committee from 2004 to 2008 and is currently the Assistant Journalist for the Historic Eastern Region of Delta Sigma Theta Sorority, Inc.

More Inspirational Quotes

"What a lovely surprise to discover how unlonely being alone can be."—*Ellen Burstyn*

"Sometimes you've got to let everything go—purge yourself. If you are unhappy with anything . . . whatever is bringing you down, get rid of it. Because you'll find that when you're free, your true creativity, your true self comes out."
—*Tina Turner*

"No time to marry, no time to settle down; I'm a young woman, and I ain't done runnin' around."—*Bessie Smith*

"That . . . man . . . says women can't have as much rights as men, 'cause Christ wasn't a woman! Where did your Christ come from? . . . From God and a woman! Man had nothing to do with Him."—*Sojourner Truth*

"The best and most beautiful things in the world cannot be seen or even touched. They must be felt with the heart."
—*Helen Keller*

"It is this belief in a power larger than myself and other than myself which allows me to venture into the unknown and even the unknowable."—*Maya Angelou*

"If you feel incomplete, you alone must fill yourself with love in all your empty, shattered spaces."—*Oprah Winfrey*

"I think the key is for women not to set any limits."
—*Martina Navratilova*

"I've learned from experience that the greater part of our happiness or misery depends on our dispositions and not on our circumstances."—*Martha Washington*

"If you want the rainbow, you've got to put up with the rain."—*Dolly Parton*

"Sometimes I feel discriminated against, but it does not make me angry. It merely astonishes me."—*Zora Neale Hurston*

"I am a feminist, and what that means to me is much the same as the meaning of the fact that I am Black: it means that I must undertake to love myself and to respect myself as though my very life depends upon self-love and self-respect."
—*June Jordan*

"He who angers you conquers you."—*Elizabeth Kenny*

"There are no shortcuts to anyplace worth going."
—*Beverly Sills*

"I love to see a young girl go out and grab the world by the lapels. Life's a bitch. You've got to go out and kick ass."
—*Maya Angelou*

"It's never too late—in fiction or life—to revise."
—*Nancy Thayer*

"If there were none who were discontent with what they have, the world would never reach for anything better."
—*Florence Nightingale*

"I keep my ideals because in spite of everything I still believe people are good at heart."—*Anne Frank*

"Should you shield the canyons from the windstorms, you would never see the true beauty of their carvings."
—*Elizabeth Kubler-Ross*

"In the space of aloneness—and perhaps only there—a woman is free to admit and act on her own desires. It is where we have the opportunity to discover that we are 'not a half' but a sovereign whole."—*Florence Falk, PhD, MSW*

CHOICES CHART

He's Gone . . . You're Back is all about recovering from the wrong relationship. Recovering from the wrong relationship is all about making the right choices.

So, instead of . . .	
Crying all day	Clean your house all day
Sleeping all the time	Pray all the time
Kicking yourself for "messing up"	Congratulate yourself for "waking up"
Drinking martinis alone on your couch	Drink peppermint tea alone in your tub
Yelling at the kids every five minutes	Hug and kiss the kids every five minutes
Working extra-long hours at the job	Work out extra hard at the gym
Wondering what your "ex" is doing	Focus on what you are doing
Burning all of his clothes and smashing the television	Donate his clothes and the television to a nearby church or organization
Beating yourself up	Pamper yourself

WORKSHOPS AND
RETREATS

A re you ready to live your life with a light heart, not a broken heart? Would you like more support in achieving this objective? It's an admirable goal and one that can be attained. But maybe you just need a little help.

Kerika Fields is committed to sharing her experiences and utilizing her information and resources to help women find the strength to move on from failed relationships. In doing so she has designed various workshops and retreats aimed at discovering what is holding you back from springing forth into your future. In addition, she is eager to speak to groups about the topic of relationship recovery.

For more information on availability for speaking engagements, workshop schedules, and retreat registration, please visit hesgoneyoureback.com.

RELATIONSHIP RECOVERY RESOURCES

LEGAL ASSISTANCE

✦ DivorceLinks.com—Provides comprehensive information on divorce laws state by state.

✦ WomansDivorce.com—Provides legal advice and help choosing divorce lawyers. Here you can download divorce forms and get information on legal separation.

✦ DivorceRecovery101.com—Online divorce recovery support group with divorce help, advice, tips, divorce law, statistics, and information.

✦ Unmarried.org—Alternatives to Marriage Project—Offers advice, information, and support for individuals who are not married under law. This site is targeted at gay/lesbian couples but provides in-depth information for anyone interested in learning his or her legal rights when it comes to cohabitation and common-law marriage. P.O. Box 320151, Brooklyn, NY 11232, phone: 718-788-1911.

- ✦ Arrearscalculator.com—Calculate how much child support you are owed and find resources to collect in a timely manner.
- ✦ LawHelp.org—This site helps low- and moderate-income people find free legal aid programs in their communities and answers to questions about their legal rights.
- ✦ Zorza.net—Zorza Associates—This legal team addresses custody, domestic violence, sexual assault, and self-help legal technology issues in an ethical and efficient manner.

MENTAL HEALTH

- ✦ 1-800-LIFENET—Mental health and substance-abuse referral agency.
- ✦ MentalHelp.net—Educate yourself about different mental health conditions.
- ✦ Jansummers.com—Licensed and experienced psychotherapist who has provided individual, family, and couples therapy for over twenty years.
- ✦ Nmha.org—Mental Health America is dedicated to diagnosing and treating mental health. Advice and resources for types of treatment and payment options.
- ✦ Dbsalliance.org—Depression and Bipolar Support Alliance—Information on depression and bipolar disorder. Also lists nationwide patient support groups. 1-800-826-3632.

✦ ABPsi.org—The Association of Black Psychologists—Guided by the principle of self-determination, these psychologists set about building an institution through which they could address mental health of the national Black community by means of planning, programs, services, training, and advocacy. P.O. Box 55999, Washington, D.C. 20040-5999, phone: 202-722-0808.

ALTERNATIVE HEATH

✦ P.E.A.C.E. Health Center—Holistic center that provides massage, acupuncture, counseling, and more. Owned and operated by licensed acupuncturist Dr. Beatrice Kinsey, phone: 718-789-3264.

✦ Sankofacenter.com—Sankofa Center for Health and Healing—Offers various healing programs, classes, and procedures for children and adults. 127 Chauncey St., Brooklyn, NY 11233, phone: 718-735-5079.

✦ Queenafuaonline.com—Healthyself Center—Owned and operated by the one and only Queen Afua, natural health advocate. Offers colonics, womb spas, fasting shut-ins, and more. Effective, alternative remedies for cleansing, detoxing, and managing female issues like fibroids, tumors, and hormonal imbalances. Also offers a great line of products, specifically Queen Afua Healing Clay. 106 Kingston Ave., Brooklyn, NY 11213, phone: 718-221-HEAL.

✦ Innervisionsworldwide.com—Inner Visions Institute for Spiritual Development—Author and life coach

Iyanla Vanzant's home base that provides spiritual counseling, ministry certificates, retreats, emotional counseling, and various workshops and programs. P.O. Box 8517, Silver Spring, MD 20907, phone: 301-419-8085.

✦ Vegcooking.com—Delicious, nutritious, and simple vegetarian recipes. This Web site is sponsored by PETA.

✦ AHHA.org—American Holistic Health Association— This Web site touts itself as being free and impartial, and it is. Information provided not promoting any one product/service but simply providing answers to your many questions about living and maintaining a holistic lifestyle.

✦ Therawfoodcoach.com—Karen Knowler provides detailed information on the benefits of raw foods. She offers help with starting and maintaining a raw food diet.

FINANCES

✦ Creditconsolidators.com—Consolidate bills. Improve your credit score.

✦ Buccs.com—Find local listings for all of your credit and budgeting needs.

✦ BCW.org—Black Career Women—Career coaching, job listings, job-hunting tips, business advice/support specifically for the Black woman. Although headquarters are in Ohio, there is a national membership network. P.O. Box 19332, Cincinnati, OH 45219-0332.

✦ Blackenterprise.com—The national magazine's Web site offers tangible advice on money management.

✦ Suzeorman.com—The financial guru's Web site provides information on investing, credit analysis, budgeting, home ownership, wills, estates, and much, much more.

CREATIVE CHILDCARE

✦ Nbcdi.org—National Black Child Development Institute, Inc.—Find programs and support that will improve the quality of life for your child. Education, mentoring, tutoring, parent empowerment, and more. Based in D.C. but has a nationwide network of members and supporters. 1313 L Street, NW, Suite 110, Washington, D.C. 20005-4110, phone: 202-833-2220.

✦ Kieto.com—Recipes, jokes, activities to share with your kids.

✦ Familycorner.com—Craft ideas, recipes, parenting tips, creative ideas for parents and children.

✦ Singlerose.com—Resources for single mothers, chat rooms, support groups, parenting advice for women raising children by choice or by change of circumstance.

✦ Creativekidsathome.com—Activities and ideas for creating arts and crafts projects with kids.